10 WEEKS TO A BETTER MARRIAGE

10 Weeks to a Better Marriage

Randall and Therese Cirner

SERVANT BOOKS
Ann Arbor, Michigan

Cover photo: Comstock
Book design by John B. Leidy

Published by
Servant Publications,
Box 8617, Ann Arbor, Michigan 48107

ISBN 0-89283-237-0
Printed in the United States of America

91   10 9 8 7 6

CONTENTS

Foreword

PERHAPS MARRIED COUPLES who are wanting to learn how to live together more happily will react to another marriage book like Liza Doolittle in *My Fair Lady*. "Words, words, words. I'm so sick of words.... Is that all you blighters can do?" Randy and Therese Cirner have anticipated this kind of reaction. They know that something more than a catalog of good advice is necessary. Their book is a plan of action, not just words. It is an invitation to action. It accompanies us as we take those actions. It recognizes how insecure and rebellious we often feel taking those actions. It encourages us. It shows us a way to walk out of destructive living patterns and habits which we do not know how to break even when we do not want to perpetuate them.

It is obvious from the present divorce rate that we need to take action. We need to learn to get along in our homes. We as a nation are proving, not that we have no love, but rather that we are pathetically poor in the skills that help us get along with each other.

There is a popular and persistent misconception abroad that those who have a good marriage just fell into it. They had the right chemistry, the right temperaments. Perhaps the main reason for this misconception is that often we believe that other people do not have problems.

Of course, differences in backgrounds and training can give certain people more living-together skills than others have. Some might have an easier combination of temperaments. We doubt, however, that there are many married couples who would not admit to having had their share of conflicts and adjustments on the road to marital compatibility. Many who are happy would say, "But we grew, we changed, we made progress." As Therese Cirner says, "It *is*: Mission Possible!"

Further, the Cirners say, "Because God is so invested in marriage he has provided for us in scripture the pattern for how the husband and wife should work together." He did not leave it up to each husband, each wife to figure out his or her own plan. He did not tell us to "do our own thing." He has told us much in scripture of how he has created marriage.

Using scripture as a basis for family-life teaching has helped many find a firm base from which to grow in family stability and happiness. Others have seen this teaching as "imposing the law." By the leading of the Holy Spirit, the New Testament writers do not shrink from laying out definite admonitions (commands, if you will) for life and faith, but they do so with the clear presupposition that they are speaking to members of a community of faith who are "abiding in Christ" and "walking in the Spirit." This book emphasizes that it is the Holy Spirit working in us who implements and realizes the commands of scripture in our life. We are not fulfilling the admonitions of scripture in our own strength; it is the work of the Holy Spirit. Commands of the Lord received and lived out in the Spirit are not oppressive *laws* but rather *promises* of what God will work in us if we trust and obey him, walking in the Spirit. These commands indicate in what direction our expectations of God should point.

This book invites us by the power of the Holy Spirit to undertake an adventure. We believe that any married couple who commit themselves to this experiment in good will and with daily dependence on the guidance and working of the Holy Spirit, will experience a deepening in unity, peace, and joy in their marriage.

LARRY AND NORDIS CHRISTENSON

Introduction

Who Is This Book For?

This book is written for Christian couples who want to deepen their marriage relationship. While non-Christians can benefit from some of the ideas and techniques we present, they will not be able to experience all the help this book offers because we base our theory and practice on two foundational principles: 1) God created marriage and has a plan for it; 2) we can know God's plan through scripture. We go to God as the source of real life in marriage. The only source for a truly successful marriage is God and his word.

We use scripture throughout the book and encourage you to read each scripture passage thoughtfully. We do not use scripture to validate or "baptize" our own ideas. Rather, our understanding of Christian marriage and how to live it practically flows from scripture. So the more you can grasp the scripture passages we cite, the easier you will find it to follow our practical and experiential suggestions.

We believe that this manual can be very helpful to most marriages.

—it can make a good marriage better

—it can make a shaky marriage more stable

—it can help a confused marriage clarify its purpose and needs

—it can put a dead-end marriage on a new path

However, this book is not *the answer* to your marriage—only God is. In fact, this book can be of only limited value to some marriages, particularly those in deep trouble. For such marriages we suggest marriage counseling from a competent Christian counselor.

Finally, we emphasize that this book is meant to be used by couples, not just by one of the partners. One partner, reading the book and following its advice, can learn some things and perhaps even make some difference in the marriage. But that misses the point of the book. Marriages can be what God intends only when both partners actively participate in his plan.

How to Use the Book

These ten weeks require active involvement on your part. This is not mainly a book of theory which can be absorbed through reading alone. It is, rather, a practical, experiential manual that requires your action if it is going to make any significant difference in your marriage. To profit fully from the book, you will need to carry out the suggestions we make at the end of each week's chapter. Go all the way. Don't fudge or cut corners or procrastinate.

Stick with it. Do one chapter a week faithfully. You are bound to encounter difficulties during the next two and a half months. You will get very busy. Perhaps you will decide you do not like to read anything. You may resist thinking or talking about things you would rather not. Don't let these concerns discourage you from continuing. Push through them and be persistent. Jump in with both feet and actively participate in the next two weeks. Give the time over to God. What have you got to lose?

Each chapter is to be covered in one week. Each chapter has three parts to it: 1) reading the chapter for the week, 2) individual time to assimilate and reflect, 3) time with your spouse for discussion and some decision-making. Our experience is that to do all three of these adequately, you should plan to take one and a half to two hours per week. The time breakdown looks something like this: 1) reading the chapter: half an hour; 2) individual time: twenty minutes to half an hour; and 3) together with spouse: forty-five minutes to one hour.

You should take individual time to reflect on the chapter right after you finish reading it. The time together can happen either on the same day or another day.

Before you begin Week One, sit down with your spouse and schedule your two hours per week for the next ten weeks. Each of you decide when to do the reading and individual activity, and then decide when to have your time together. Get out a calendar and write it down so you won't forget. Make the necessary arrangements for your hours together to be private, just the two of you without interruptions.

At the end of the ten weeks you should take a weekend away. Because of job considerations, baby-sitters, and other time commitments, now is not too soon to schedule the weekend. It doesn't have to be right after you finish the manual, but should be reasonably close to it. We think you will find it a fitting wrap-up to the ten weeks you spent going through the book.

Finally, remember that marriage is a lifelong commitment that requires lifelong work. This ten-week program is not a crash course that you can do and then forget. It can help your marriage. But after you finish this book, you need to continue to pay attention to your life together!

Don't hesitate to use this book over and over again in different ways. What we present here are marriage basics, things we all need to be reminded of periodically. Every three or four months pick a chapter to read again and talk about together. This is a good way to keep from sliding back into old, unwanted habits.

Our prayer for you is that God will greatly enrich and strengthen your marriage and will give you the joy and peace he desires you to have.

Other Books You Will Find Helpful

Larry and Nordis Christenson, *The Christian Couple* (Minneapolis: Bethany Fellowship, 1977).

Ralph Martin, *Husbands, Wives, Parents, Children* (Ann Arbor: Servant Books, 1978).

We have also recommended readings at the ends of some chapters.

Week One

Who Is in Charge?

STOP! If you are one of those people who don't read the introduction to books, you missed something this time. Please go back and read it. It will only take ten minutes—honest.

OUR YOUNG FRIENDS Rob and June got married out of rebellion. They were both young, just out of high school. Rob was thinking of going on to college, and June was looking for a job. They had been dating for only about a year and had been experiencing increased pressure from their parents to break off the relationship. Rob's parents didn't want anything to interfere with his schooling, and they were afraid an early marriage would mean the end of college. June's parents didn't particularly care for the relationship because they felt that June could find a better match than Rob.

Rob and June decided to "show them" and got married sooner than even they had intended. After they were married, Rob and June began to discover that they really didn't know one another very well. They had been bonded together by a common "enemy" before marriage—their parents. Now that the pressure was off, they had a chance to really look at one another and weren't sure they liked what they saw. Difficulties began; the relationship grew stormier and stormier, ending finally in divorce. Though not all marriages based on rebellion end in divorce, this one did.

Why Did You Get Married?

Many of us can answer this question right away. Others may have to stop and think for a moment, going back over the years, trying to put into words something which by now may be only a dim memory of a far-off feeling. But we all had reasons, whether we remember clearly or not. Here are some of the more common reasons people get married. Do any of them sound familiar?

1. Fell in love
2. Sexual desire (it contributes greatly to #1)
3. Fear of loneliness or rejection (all my friends were getting married and I didn't want to be left behind)
4. Security
5. Money or prestige
6. Everybody just expected we would marry one another
7. Premarital pregnancy left little choice
8. Rebellion
9. It just seemed like the right thing to do

While most people get married for these reasons, we need to ask the question, "Are these the right reasons?" Or perhaps a better way to phrase the question is: "Do these reasons get to the heart of what marriage is all about?" Christians, who know that God created marriage and has a purpose for it, must answer no. These reasons, the reasons most people get married, fail to recognize the true context for marriage in God's plan—namely, that marriage is a way we live out our basic Christian commitment.

All Christians, whether married or single, are commanded to live a life of love and service to God and our Christian brothers and sisters and to bring the good news of the gospel of Christ to the world around us. How many of you had this as part of your reason for getting married? How many of your friends saw this love and service as a reason for marriage? Not many, we bet.

The fact that few people get married for the right reasons isn't surprising. One of the great tragedies is that Christians look to the secular world for models of marriage. While God is the one who created marriage, blessed it, and made a plan for it, where do we look when we want to know what marriage is all about? We look to our friends, our relatives, parents, television, movies, famous people, "experts," and advice-givers. Some of these people have valuable things to say, especially if they are speaking from a Christian perspective. For the most part however, the media, famous people, and experts give us a very anemic and myopic view of marriage.

The world's view has little in common with the Christian view, and since the world is what forms most Christians' understanding of marriage, it's little wonder that marriage among Christians today is in such sad shape. If we sow the world's seed, we will reap the world's harvest. Divorce rates among Christians are only a little better than among non-Christians. That means that divorce among Christians is approaching the 50 percent rate.

Marriage is supposed to be a way we live out our basic Christian commitment, not an escape from it or an exception to it. Only by reintegrating the two will Christians have the right perspective from which to see God's reasons for marriage and have a solid base on which to build a successful one.

What are God's reasons (his plan) for marriage? We think they can be summed up this way:
   1. To become one flesh
   2. For committed love
   3. For mutual service
Let's look at each of these more closely.

1. To become one flesh. The main purpose of marriage is to create a new entity—the family. It begins with a man and a woman giving up their individual lives to form a new one together. It is no longer *my* life but *our* life. It is a union of commitment and permanence just like the union between Christ and the church, which the Apostle Paul says is the model for Christian marriage.

" 'For this reason a man shall leave his father and mother and be joined to his wife, and the two shall become one flesh.' This mystery is a profound one, and I am saying that it refers to Christ and the church" (Eph 5:31-32).

Out of the sexual union come children, whom scripture calls both a blessing from God (Ps 127 and Ps 128) and also a duty or responsibility of the husband and wife (Gn 1:28). Children are a new generation of God's sons and daughters meant for eternal life with him and fruitful labor for him on earth.

2. For committed love. It sounds obvious to say that marriage is for committed love. But too many people confuse the abiding love of commitment and service, which is God's plan, with the fickleness of infatuation and changing emotions, which the world around us says is love. We will talk concretely about this in chapter four.

3. For mutual service. The idea that marriage is for mutual service certainly runs counter to the prevailing notions in today's Western society, permeated as it is with self: self-concern, self-fulfillment, self-protection, self-importance. And yet, being servants of one another is a very clear and consistent theme in the New Testament. Scripture holds up Jesus as *the* ideal servant and calls his disciples to walk the same path. In chapters six and seven we will see how husbands and wives can serve one another.

Hope for Marriages

Some of you probably have recognized by now a disparity between why you *did* get married and why you *should* have gotten married. Perhaps condemnation or discouragement have set in, and you are tempted to toss this book in the trash. Perhaps the ideal presented sounds beyond you, and you don't see how you can possibly get there. Welcome to the club. Not many people did have this all figured out when they got married, and certainly no one can get there on his or her own power. Whatever you do, don't close the book. Read on because there is hope for your marriage.

We had occasion to observe the marriage of another young couple that turned out very differently than the one which began the chapter. Frank and Tina were the classic case of the "perfect match" high-school sweethearts. Physically attractive, athletic, popular—the whole school just expected they would get married. Shortly after graduation, Frank and Tina obliged their schoolmates and got married. They too discovered they were hurried into marriage and had to get acquainted with one another in ways they hadn't realized. Just like Rob and June, Frank and Tina found that they had all the elements present for a tumultuous and perhaps tragic marriage.

But something happened to Frank and Tina—they both came into a personal relationship with Jesus Christ. They submitted both their personal lives and their marriage to him in the realization that God was the only one capable of giving them the help and strength they needed. Today, nearly ten years later, they have a strong, committed relationship, a number of beautiful, Christian children, and have served as an example to other young married couples of the power and faithfulness of God.

Why did Frank and Tina fare better than Rob and June? Both marriages had obvious strengths and weaknesses right from the beginning. Both couples were young, inexperienced, blind to most things, knowing mainly that they wanted one another—and not even sure what that meant, except perhaps sexually. Why did Frank and Tina "make it"?

Frank and Tina made it because something, or better someone, broke into their lives and offered them a way to have a successful marriage. This couple discovered God's plan for marriage and decided to take it on. Frank and Tina realized that they had made a start in marriage based on the only foundations they knew. But they were perceptive enough to know that those foundations were not enough to see them through the years to come. When they encountered God's plan, they recognized that here was hope, strength, joy, peace, and they went after it. This young couple discovered what we call the three Christian truths of marriage:

1. God created marriage and has a plan for it
2. Husband and wife need to admit their need for God's plan
3. Husband and wife need God's help to live his plan

Much of what follows in this book is an elaboration of what Frank and Tina discovered. Let's examine each of these truths more carefully.

Marriage Is God's Design

God created marriage and has a plan for it which he has made known to us in scripture. Marriage is God's purpose and not simply a human invention to meet a societal need. Secular thinking views marriage (and, by extension, family life) as purely human. The famous futurist Alvin Toffler, for example, sees marriage as an ever-changing function of technological society.

As human relationships grow more transient and modular, the pursuit of love becomes, if anything, more frenzied. But the temporal expectations change. As conventional marriage proves itself less and less capable of delivering on its promise of lifelong love, therefore, we can anticipate open public acceptance of temporary marriages. Instead of wedding "until death do us part," couples will enter into matrimony knowing from the first that the relationship is likely to be short-lived.

They will know, too, that when the paths of husband and wife diverge, when there is too great a discrepancy in developmental stages, they may call it quits—without shock or embarrassment, perhaps even without some of the pain that goes with divorce today. And when the opportunity presents itself, they will marry again . . . and again . . . and again. (*Future Shock,* p. 251)

Feminists also fail to recognize God's sovereignty in marriage. They see marriage as something to be shaped to their own liking and designs. Here is what Betty Friedan, the feminist theorist, says:

I believe that feminism must, in fact, confront the family, albeit in new terms, if the movement is to fulfill its own revolutionary function in modern society. Otherwise it will abort or be put on history's shelf—its real promise and significance obscured, distorted, by its denial of life's realities for too many millions of women. Locked into reaction against women's role in the family of the past, we could blindly emulate an obsolete narrow male role in corporate bureaucracy which seems to have more power, not understanding that the power and the promise of the future lie in transcending that absolute separation of the sex roles, in work and family.

"But to confront the American family as it actually is today, instead of hysterically defending or attacking the family of Western nostalgia," as Stanford sociologist William J. Goode calls it—means shattering an icon that is still sacred to both church and state. And dispelling the mystique of the family seems to be even more threatening to some than unmasking the feminine mystique was for so many a decade ago. But it is that obsolete image of the family that polarizes and paralyzes our power to solve the new problems, politically and personally. (*The Second Stage,* pp. 84, 99)

Marriage in the secular model, whether futurist or feminist, is doomed to frustration and failure because it doesn't recognize the true designer of marriage—God.

Other people, including some Christians, make the mistake of seeing techniques as the secret to a successful marriage—techniques for communicating, decision making, lovemaking, parenting, etc. Some of these techniques are helpful, in fact, very valuable aids in marriage, and we will be presenting a good many practical helps in this book. Techniques, however, as good as they may be, are not the "secret" of a happy marriage. They are not the source of a successful marriage. God is.

We Need God

Husband and wife together need to admit their need for God's plan for marriage. We can enter into the fullness of Christian marriage only when the husband and wife are walking in it together. It won't work with one partner trying it alone. If one partner cannot fully accept God's plan, you can still have a good marriage, but you won't enjoy the richness of his life and grace which come from living his plan together. It would be like trying to run a three-legged race when one person doesn't have his heart fully into the race. That team will make progress down the field and perhaps will even cross the finish line, but it won't be an easy race—nor a very graceful one. That's the way Christian marriage is. The spouses are bound together in life much more securely and intimately than any partners in a three-legged race. One can't run without the other. That is the way God intended it.

If husband and wife are going to enter God's plan together, they cannot point fingers.

"I'm doing basically O.K., *he* is the one who really needs to change."

"If she would just do what I tell her, things would be all right."

Instead, the fundamental attitude each should take is "how can you say to your brother, 'Let me take the speck out of your eye,' when there is the log in your own eye? ... first take the log out of your own eye, and then you will see clearly to take the speck out of your brother's eye" (Mt 7:4-5).

A number of years ago, I (Randy) spent some months counseling Jim and Marge. Jim took the initiative to get help and Marge was willing. At our first meeting, I asked them to describe the problems they were facing. Jim launched into a detailed description of what he saw as the problem. It all boiled down to one thing—Marge. After he finished, I asked if there wasn't something else contributing to the problem. After a moment he said there wasn't.

I knew these two well, and I knew that Jim saw some real problems in Marge. But I also knew that he had failed to mention his own lack of self-discipline and inconsistency which contributed greatly to Marge's inability to gain control over her difficulties. I pointed out to Jim that until he saw his own part in these problems, he would never see the changes in Marge that he wanted to see. As Jim came to grips with his own part in the problem, both he and Marge were able to overcome many long-standing problems.

It is always easier to see our spouse's problems and faults than our own. But we urge you, right from the beginning of this book, to recognize that none of us is perfect and together admit your corporate need for God's plan in your marriage.

God's Power

We can't live God's plan for our marriage on our own power. The Christian life calls us to high ideals. Seen by themselves, these ideals doom us to failure before we begin. I remember early in our marriage both of us thought that we would never attain the level of Christian marriage held out to us in scripture. We are both just too independent, opinionated, and stubborn, among other things. Even if one of us could change, we were sure the other never would. We were absolutely right. On our own, neither of us could make the lasting changes we needed, even though we tried very hard.

The good news about God's life is that we live it through the power of God. The Holy Spirit is at work in us to bring about the life of God in ever deeper measure. And it is the power of the Holy Spirit which enables us to have the rich, joy-filled marriage God intends for us.

No matter what your reasons for getting married, no matter how badly you think you've botched it, even if you are divorced and remarried, there is hope and help for you through the power of God. Even "after all these years," when you think you are set in your ways, God's power can work in your life. Even though you have made mistakes (maybe lots of them), God can renew your marriage. Despite the hurts you have consciously or unconsciously inflicted on one another, God can heal your relationship and make it stronger than ever. Such is the power of God—if we are willing to accept it. It's humbling to have to admit that we need help, but once we do God can begin to work.

As we reach out to God and he begins to act in our marriage, there are two very important things we need to do in order to cooperate with his work.

Prayer

The greatest spiritual tools we Christians have for drawing close to God and receiving his help are prayer and scripture. As you enter this ten-week adventure, come before God with faith in his ability and desire to work in your marriage. Ask him to help you make the changes you need. Scripture promises us that God hears and answers our prayers.

"Ask, and it will be given you; seek, and you will find; knock, and it will be opened to you. For everyone who asks receives, and he who seeks finds, and to him who knocks it will be opened" (Mt 7:7-8).

Decide to take time every day during the ten weeks you work through this book to bring your marriage before the Lord in prayer together. Pray in whatever way you feel most comfortable: conversationally, silently, reading a psalm which asks God's favor, praying in the Spirit, praying the Lord's Prayer. *The important thing is to do it.* If you are not used to praying together, then pray alone for a couple of weeks. After you have worked through some of the chapters that follow, you may find yourselves more comfortable praying together.

Perseverance

The second thing you can do to be open to God's action in your marriage is to keep at it. Continue to put into practice what you learn in this book even though it seems difficult. God's action in our lives is not always or even primarily characterized by instantaneous change. Often, rather, we find habits and patterns and attitudes changing bit by bit as we persevere, trusting in God's action.

None of the truly successful marriages we know of came about overnight. There was much hard work, personal sacrifice, and determination to make it work. Our own marriage is strong; it took time and work, and it is all worth it. We urge you to not give up until you have come fully into God's plan for your marriage. Let him be in charge of it.

Marriage is not a private affair. It is not simply a matter of the two of you making your own decisions and plans, building your own hopes and dreams. The reason so many marriages today (even between Christians) are in trouble, or dead-ended in boredom is that the partners have tried to make the marriage work on their own. That is precisely the problem. God never intended marriage to be like that. Marriage is not supposed to be a one-to-one relationship, but a threesome. Not the threesome of popular, secular love songs where one spouse has a secret "love-affair" with someone else. The real and necessary triangle is the one in which God is an acknowledged member. Without him no marriage will ever be the success it can be.

The title of this chapter asks the question, Who is in charge? Who is in charge of your marriage? You? Your spouse? Money? Sex? Rebellion? Fear? God is the one who wants to be—and should be. Give it to him.

To Do This Week

Each of you should answer the questions separately, then come back together and discuss your answers. Since you will be doing this for each week of the program, you should write your answers in separate notebooks.

Individual Time

Answer the questions:

1. Why did I (we) get married? If you have more than one reason, rank them in order of importance to you.

Fell in love _____	Expectations _____
Sexual desire _____	Rebellion _____
Loneliness _____	Pregnancy _____
Need for security _____	Have a Christian marriage _____
Money _____	Serve God together _____
Prestige _____	Other _____

2. What has been most influential in forming my idea of what marriage should be?

Parents _____	Movies _____
Friends _____	My church _____
T.V. _____	Scripture _____
Books _____	Other _____

3. Am I satisfied with where our marriage is?

4. What would I most like to see change?

5. Am I ready to make God the third partner in our marriage and live according to his plan for it?

Yes _____	I think so, what do you think? _____
No _____	Willing but scared _____

If you have been a nominal Christian, we recommend that you make a personal commitment to Jesus Christ right now, asking him to renew and empower your life. If you have a hard time doing it in your own words, here is a prayer you can use.

Jesus, I acknowledge that I haven't lived my life as you want me to. I've sinned against you, my [husband, wife], my children, and I ask your forgiveness. I want you to be the center of my life. I acknowledge you as my Lord and Savior. Fill me now with your Holy Spirit and empower me to live my life fully for you.

Time Together

1. Share your answers to the above questions with one another.

2. If you both want God's plan for your marriage, commit yourselves to it now through the following dialogue. Make up your own if you wish.

Husband: (wife's name), I want to improve our marriage by basing it more on God's plan. I commit myself to taking these ten weeks as a way to do that. I'll seek God's help and do my best because I love you and want the best for our marriage.

Wife: same as above, using husband's name.

Let's Talk about It: Communication I

THERE IS A STORY about an old couple who had been married nearly seventy years. Edna, the wife, now ninety years old, was dying. She lay in a hospital bed while John, her husband, sat by her side. Edna said, "You know, John, we have had a good life together. I'm ready to die and have no fears. I do have one regret about our marriage, though, and that is that you never told me that you loved me."

John looked surprised, and then replied, "Why Edna! I told you on our wedding day that I loved you and said that if I ever changed my mind I would let you know."

Whether you find the above story humorous or grim, you will have to admit that something was lacking in John and Edna's relationship—communication. Communication can be one of the most fruitful relationship-building activities of your marriage. Do you believe that? If you don't, we can probably tell you why. It's because most of your experiences with communicating with one another have been negative ones. How many of the following characterize your attempts to talk to one another?

Nagging	Accusing
Complaining	Demanding
Anger	Criticizing
Dumping	Putting-down
Blaming	Distraction

Who wants to talk when this is what happens? Certainly not the person on the receiving end. And since most people can't resist giving tit for tat, both of you are on the receiving end. Small wonder that "communication" is a dirty word in some homes.

Jim and Marge, the couple we met in the last chapter, almost never talked to one another beyond the purely functional necessities such as "Pass the salt" or "Where are you going?" Jim was afraid to say anything more serious because Marge would begin complaining about whatever the topic might be. Money was a major issue for Marge. She was determined not to let their family get caught in some financial backwater. She wanted money and the things money could buy, and she was constantly nagging Jim about money. He wouldn't bring the subject up even if he had something to say because he didn't want to get Marge started. Once Marge got going, however, Jim was ready to tell her what a problem she had. And away they would go, around and around until they lost sight of the original issue. Since this happened repeatedly in most areas of their life together, for the sake of peace, Jim and Marge eventually drifted into the pattern of not talking at all.

The Need for Communication

Communication is meant to be a blessing in marriage, not a difficulty. It is supposed to help us keep in touch and support our life together as husband and wife. It fills three critical needs in marriage.

1. Communication supports our love relationship. Remember that we said last week that marriage is not simply a functional invention of changing social structures. It's God's plan for his sons and daughters. It's supposed to be a love relationship founded on the love of Christ which we have for one another.

Communication with our spouse is an important means of growing in our love for one another. As we talk about the many areas of our personal and corporate life together and make decisions and plans, our sense of commitment and care for one another grows and deepens. It is difficult to grow in your love for someone if you never see them or talk to them.

Think about some of your relatives, for example. When you were a child, living with your parents, there were probably some relatives (aunts, uncles, cousins) whom you visited pretty frequently. As you did so, your relationship with them grew. You got to know them, and, in your child's way, had a love and concern for them. As you grew older, left home, perhaps moved to a different city or state or country, got married, and began raising a family, you had less and less contact with some (maybe even all) of your relatives. Perhaps you lost contact with some of your relatives altogether; others you may still be in contact with through letters or phone calls or even periodic visits.

While you still love all your relatives, you probably feel closest to those you have contact with. In fact, the more frequent and meaningful the contact, the deeper the relationship. You still love those you haven't had contact with since you were fifteen years old, but you can't say that your relationship has grown over the years. *You* have grown, and *they* have grown, but your relationship together hasn't grown. In short, meaningful contact with another person is essential if your relationship is to grow. Communication is an essential part of "meaningful contact."

2. Communication keeps the machinery running smoothly.

Scene: Cirner home, Tuesday afternoon
Characters: Real names used so that justice may be served

Randy (coming downstairs from home office): "Therese, do you have the keys to the car?"

Therese (putting coat on): "They are in my purse, why?"

Randy (eyeing coat suspiciously): "I have a meeting I have to be at in twenty minutes on the other side of town."

Therese (zips up coat): "Oh, well, I have a doctor's appointment for Rebecca now. I can be back in an hour."

Randy (fiddling with his Day-Timer): "Won't do. There are five other people involved, all with tight schedules. I can't change it this late. Can you drop me off and I'll get a ride home?"

Therese (reaching for purse where keys are): "Where is the meeting?"

Randy (still fiddling): "North Maple."

Therese (purse now safely within her grasp): "Hmmmm. I don't think I have time. I can just barely make the appointment now. North Maple is fifteen minutes in the opposite direction."

Randy (jaw muscles begin to twitch slightly): "Why didn't you tell me sooner you had an appointment for Rebecca?"

Therese (gathering baby into her arms): "I just made it this morning. Remember, she was up half the night crying. I'm pretty sure it's an ear infection. She needs a prescription. I didn't know you had a meeting this afternoon. We missed our planning time yesterday morning."

Randy (muscle twitch greatly pronounced): "I know. The car had to be fixed. That was the only time I could take it to the garage."

The scene ended without bloodshed or tears, but no one was happy. Randy was late for his meeting and had to get a ride home from people who didn't live anywhere near him. Therese was late for the doctor because she drove Randy to his meeting, and since other patients were now ahead of her, it took even longer to see the doctor. Rebecca, however, got her prescription and began feeling much better.

Many daily practical things such as the conflicting car needs are part of marriage. How those things get handled can make the difference between a peaceful day and a hectic day. Every day in the Cirner house is not like the one described above. In fact such scenes are rare. The right kind of forethought and planning can make them infrequent for you too. You see, we have found that sitting down together at the beginning of the week and planning the week—checking schedules, noting conflicts, anticipating problems—makes all the difference. The practical events of a busy and fast-paced week receive the necessary planning before they begin to happen. The result is a peaceful and ordered practical home life. We will talk more about how to do this type of scheduling a little later in the chapter.

3. Communication gives a time and place for handling problems. It isn't always easy to find the right kind of time to discuss the problems or major issues that arise in marriage, so we often make the mistake of trying to talk about them when we shouldn't. Do *not* discuss problems

    —at the dinner table with the kids present

    —at a quiet restaurant (especially if you plan on going there again)

    —when one of you is about to go out the door somewhere

    —when you are really steamed up

    —when other people are present

    —*never, never, never* while in bed going to sleep

    —right after one of you comes home from a long, hard day

We will say more about when to talk about problems in a minute. The important thing is to have a time set aside to talk about problems so that you don't have to always shoot from the hip. Communication in marriage isn't an *option;* it's a *necessity.*

Getting It to Happen

Once we agree to the need for communication in our marriage, how do we get it to happen? The answer is, the same way you get anything important to happen. If you both wanted to go to a play, or a concert, or a friend's wedding, or an antique show, or watch the Super Bowl, how would you get it to happen? You would note the event on your calendar and not let anything else interfere with it. If a friend asked you to play golf, you would decline because the other activity was more important to you. If a friend called on the phone as you were leaving, you would excuse yourself and offer to call back later. In a word, you would make that desired activity a *priority.*

That is how we ensure that communication takes place: we make it a priority. If you aren't willing to make communication a priority, it will not happen. You may talk to each other about important matters periodically, but you will never have the regularity and consistency you need if communication is to make a decisive difference in your relationship.

In our marriage, we make sure that our communication time together is right near the top of the priorities in our weekly schedule. Over the years, we have found this time together to be so beneficial that we wouldn't dream of returning to the catch-as-catch-can method.

Once you have decided that communication is a priority, you move it from theory to reality in three steps.

Step 1: Set the time. Don't just agree to talk "sometime this week." You won't get to it. Be specific. Thursday evening 7:30; Saturday morning 10:00. Write it down. Block it out on the calendar. We highly recommend that you choose a time that is the most peaceful time of the day for both of you. What works best for us right now is 9:00 A.M. Monday. The three older kids are off to school, and the two younger ones haven't been awake long enough to be bored playing with their toys or watching Mister Rogers. The telephone calls haven't hit full stride yet. Both of us are fresh. It's an ideal time. It is possible for us because our work schedules are flexible.

We have discovered that certain times don't work very well. One is late afternoon after Randy finishes his work day. This time may work for some couples, but it is bad for us.

Another bad time is late at night, just before going to bed. We are both just too tired to put much effort into communication at that particular time. Most other couples we know agree that late night is not a good time. Tired people are usually more irritable and sensitive. You may find that trying to discuss a minor problem quickly moves to the level of an international incident.

Step 2: Find the right place. Finding the right place to talk is as important as setting a time. There are some places which are just not conducive to having a fruitful conversation. You won't communicate very well (at least not with each another) if you try to talk in the living room while all the children are around—even if they "promise" not to interrupt you. Nor will you be able to accomplish much if you try to communicate anything substantial while you do something else, such as bowling, shopping, painting the living room, or watching television.

The only way you will have a consistently fruitful communication time is to do it in a place where you are able to give one another your undivided attention, with as little distraction as possible. Here are some places we and our friends have found to be effective.

—In a quiet part of the house when the kids are gone or in bed and the phone is unplugged

—During a walk in the woods

—At a picnic table in a park

—While taking a leisurely ride in the country

People with young children will find that often the only way to get their talking done is to get a babysitter and go out. If you have young children, it is well worth the few dollars you will spend on a sitter to have the time together you need.

Step 3: Do it often enough. How often you have your communication time will depend somewhat on your particular circumstances. If your life is complex, your children are older, and you have a backlog of problems to talk through, you will need more time for communication than newlyweds.

Generally, our experience with marriages across the spectrum, is that there should be a specific communication time *every week* for about one and a half hours. This amount of time seems to meet the normal range of needs all married couples encounter. With changing circumstances, however, you may want to cut back to one hour a week or increase your time either by lengthening the time you spend once a week or by establishing a second communication time. If you need more time, *schedule it!*

We don't recommend trying to get by on less than one to one and a half hours *each week*. No matter what your circumstances are, you surely have enough to talk about to cover that time. Remember that the goal here is *not* to cut communication to a minimum, but to provide a time *and* an environment where you and your spouse can be together and grow in your relationship. In this area of your life, less is definitely *not* better.

At the same time, *quality* of communication is more important than *quantity*. If you spend five hours a week in "communication time" together but engage in mostly idle chatter or neighborhood gossip, you have missed the point. It's more fruitful to spend less time, but spend it in a disciplined manner. In short, try to get the time you need and use the time as productively as possible.

Now, you find yourselves at 8:30 on Tuesday evening sitting across from one another in a little coffee shop waiting for your cheesecake to be served. What do you talk about?

What to Talk About

In the couples worksheet at the end of this chapter we have included a detailed checklist of items for you and your spouse to be in communication about. We want to list here only the broad categories and give a few words of orientation. You won't always have something to talk about in every category each week. The list includes the main things most couples should be in regular touch about. We have found, for example, that we need to talk about finances only twice a month—a mid-month review and an end-of-month wrap-up, which includes looking ahead to the new month. As long as you *both* feel that you are in good touch with one another in particular areas, you can talk about them twice a month, once a month, and maybe even less. The checklist is a reminder, not a law.

We put the items in the checklist in the order we think is best to deal with them. Practical items which can be dealt with quickly are first so we can get them out of the way. Items that have to do with our personal lives or those that will require some discussion get handled after the practical things.

A simple communication checklist looks like this:

—Events for coming week

—Physical needs for home
  (work projects, chores)

—Miscellaneous items (guests)

—Finances

—Children

—Our personal lives

—Problems

—Prayer

The last item on the checklist is prayer. We recommend that your communication times end with a short time of prayer, asking God's continued blessing on your marriage and family, and asking his help with the problems, difficulties, and concerns you face. After all, it is his grace and power we are supposed to rely on, not our own. Prayer together reminds us of this and places our marriage right where it is meant to be—in his hands.

"Have no anxiety about anything, but in everything by prayer and supplication with thanksgiving let your requests be made known to God. And the peace of God, which passes all understanding, will keep your hearts and your minds in Christ Jesus" (Phil 4:6-7).

Finally, both of you should come to your time together with the things you want to discuss. If there is too much to talk about, prioritize your lists, discuss the most important items, and leave the rest until next time. Both of you should come prepared and ready to actively participate. The husband shouldn't come expecting his wife to do all the talking, and the wife shouldn't come expecting her husband to be sensitive enough always to ask her just the right questions.

To Do This Week

Individual Time

Answer the questions:
1. Did I pray for our marriage this week?

2. How do I rate our communication?

Excellent _____   Poor _____

Good _____   Nonexistent _____

So-So _____

3. What are the things I feel the greatest need to talk about? Make a list in order of importance.

4. What do I think is the greatest obstacle to our having good communication?

Busyness _____   Me _____

Kids _____   Laziness _____

Television _____   Other _____

Time Together

1. Share your answers to the above questions with one another.

2. Using both your lists from question three above, establish a common priority list of things you need to talk about.

3. Taking into account your answers to question four above, use the

schedule below to establish a regular one-and-a-half-hour communication time each week for the next month. Write the time under the appropriate day each week. Make a commitment to actually take the time designated. *Do it.*

Week	M	T	W	Th	F	Sa	Su
1							
2							
3							
4							

4. Pray that God will bless your communication.

Communication Checklist

Here is a more detailed list of areas to address in your time together. Remember, not everything needs to be touched each week. The breakdown of the checklist reflects our experience with how often things need to be discussed. Your needs and desires may indicate a slightly different arrangement than we have here.

Weekly

Schedule

____ husband's and wife's personal activities

____ communication time

____ time together (see week six)

____ children's schedule

____ family activities

____ other events

____ resolve time and transportation conflicts

Home

_____ chores for family members   _____ any problems (squeaky doors, broken locks, etc.)

Finances

_____emergency or unexpected needs

Husband's and wife's lives

_____ Keep each other in touch with events at work and home and neighborhood   _____Problems or issues in your relationship or family life which need resolution

Other

_____ Any other immediate concerns not covered in the checklist   _____End with prayer

Bi-weekly

In addition to the weekly things, you should discuss the following.

Finances

_____ End of month or beginning of month review   _____ Mid-month check: are we living within our means? what needs do we have for the rest of the month?

Husband-wife relationship

_____ Share what each is doing in prayer and scripture

Monthly

Children

_____ How each child is doing

_____ Relationships among brothers and sisters

_____ How is discipline working

_____ School: academics and problems

_____ What training is being done

_____ Plan to spend time with them

In addition to the above areas, you should occasionally do some long-range planning of such things as: holidays, vacations, family-time planning, financial needs, saving for college, retirement, debts.

As you can see, the monthly items to be discussed can be sizable. If you find that you can't do it in one and a half hours, be sure to plan on taking longer. Most of these areas won't collapse if you miss talking about them occasionally, but don't slip into the habit of letting them slide.

For further reading:

H. Norman Wright, *Communication: Key to Your Marriage* (Glendale, Calif.: Regal Books, 1974).

Week Three

"Let No Evil Talk": Communication II

A S WE SAW LAST WEEK, regular communication can be a tremendous benefit to a successful marriage. For some couples, the problem is not so much knowing *what* to talk about but knowing *how* to talk about it. Wrong ways of speaking to one another can torpedo even the simplest discussion. This week we want to look at some of the more important dos and don'ts of good communication. Some things we discuss here are simply techniques for good communication. However, much of what we present is not just technique, but rather scriptural teaching about speech. We go beyond saying, "Here is a helpful way . . ." to saying, "Here is how *God* says we must . . . ." For example, it is helpful and very polite to maintain eye contact during communication. But if you look at your shoes instead of your spouse, you are not sinning. On the other hand, if you lie to your spouse or let anger rule your conversation, you are sinning and need to repent.

Here is a list of the more important dos and don'ts of communication.

Do	Right	Wrong
Be straightforward and clear.	"I think we need to talk more often about finances so I can help you keep track of the checkbook balance."	"The checkbook is overdrawn again. 'Somebody' isn't paying proper attention to the balance."
Be patient.	"I can see that you are pretty concerned about how much television the kids watch. Let's work it out."	"Why are you always harping about how much T.V. the kids watch?"
Be attentive, listen.	Eye contact, face each other at close range.	Sit on opposite sides of the room, constantly glance at watch; do crossword puzzle; clean out tackle box.
Understand what spouse is saying.	"Let me see if I understand. You are saying that if the only time I show you physical affection is during lovemaking, you find it hard to respond. Is that right?"	"Look, men and women are different. Besides we can't walk around all day holding hands."
Acknowledge that your perception about something can be wrong.	"I could be wrong, but it seems to me that you are losing your commitment to our communication time."	"You don't want to spend time with me, do you? You would rather stay home and read. Admit it!"
Accept responsibility for your wrongdoing and ask forgiveness.	"You are right, I did say that and it was wrong. I'm sorry, will you forgive me?" Answer: "I forgive you."	"What *I* said wrong! You should talk. You started the whole thing in the first place. I just followed your lead. *You* stop what *you* are doing and *I* won't be a 'problem.'"

Don't	Wrong	Right
Dump.	"Things are lousy, and I'd better get some relief. The kids are unruly, your darn dog barks all day long, food disappears from the shelves faster than I can buy it, and you are doing a bunch of things that bug the heck out of me."	"I'm not doing so hot. There are some things going on that bother me and I'm not sure how to get them resolved. I'll do my best to explain what they are, but I may get a little emotional about it."
Be defensive.	"I do *not* spend too much time fishing. I have little enough time to myself. Anyway, I work hard and need some relaxation."	"I don't think I spend too much time fishing. On the other hand, I don't want to neglect any of my responsibilities. Let's examine it some more."
Expect an answer to every problem or need.	"How are you going to solve our money problems, huh? Just tell me that. Where are we going to get money to buy the kids' school clothes, where? How can we afford to visit mother at the end of the summer? These things are important. What are you going to do about them?"	"I realize we have some significant money needs coming up shortly—like the kids' school clothes. I'd hoped we could visit my mother. Money is tight right now. I'd like to talk about how to approach these needs. I have to admit, my anxiety level is pretty high."
Use "always" or "never."	"You never take me out to dinner." "You are always complaining."	"It's been awhile since we have been out to dinner. Let's go soon." "You may not realize it, but you complain quite a bit. In fact, complaining about something makes it harder to deal with the issue."

Don't	Wrong	Right
Call into question spouse's basic love and commitment to you.	"If you really love me, how can you say what you just did? This says more about what you think than all the I love yous you've spoken."	"What you just said was very hard for me to hear."
Force your spouse to deal with something they aren't ready to deal with.	"Look. This is an important issue—important to me, anyway, and I want us to talk about it right now."	"It looks like you aren't ready to talk about this right now so let's put it off for a week or two. But I think it is important, and I would like to discuss it soon."
Have to be right.	Load all your guns; dig in; refuse to budge; invest your *self* in the issue; shoot down anything your spouse says.	Recognize the reasonableness of the other's position; have a teachable spirit; if the issue is not a matter of moral right and wrong, see that unity and peace are more important than the issue—or your ego.

Other don'ts: don't use sarcasm; don't bring up the past (unless it's a matter for reconciliation—then get reconciled and forget it); don't interrupt; don't walk out in anger; don't use emotional manipulation; don't use the silent treatment; don't use nonverbal interruptions (sighs, frowns, shrugs, finger-tapping, etc.).

Communication is a two-way street, involving give and take in sharing and listening. Each partner has the responsibility to behave righteously. By what we say and the way we say it, we can determine the course and tone of our conversation. God gives us some very good wisdom about speech in scripture. Here is a sampling from Proverbs.

"There is one whose rash words are like sword thrusts, but the tongue of the wise brings healing" (Prv 12:18).

"A soft answer turns away wrath, but a harsh word stirs up anger" (Prv 15:1).

"Pleasant words are like a honeycomb, sweetness to the soul and health to the body" (Prv 16:24).

Both partners in a marriage need to make a commitment to righteous speech and action. One partner trying on his or her own won't get very far.

Men and Women Are Different

Although some people deny it, God made men and women different. He didn't make one sex better than the other, just different. He made us different so that men and women, husbands and wives, can fulfill differing responsibilities. These differences show us how men and women think, speak, and act. The differences aren't absolutes, but we can say that men or women "tend" to show different traits. If we have a basic appreciation for these differences and how they affect communication, we will be better able to overcome some misunderstandings and allow for more realistic expectations for our communication. We will also be in a better position to serve our spouse's needs.

There are many differences between men and women which we will discuss more at length in Week Nine. For now we want to look at one difference which has a significant effect on communication.

Difference: Women tend to relate more on a verbal level, while men tend to relate more out of camaraderie.

A number of years ago we had an experience which exemplifies this point.

I (Randy) hadn't been fishing for a while, so I called my friend Bill and arranged to get away on a Saturday morning for some bass fishing down on the pond. He picked me up a little before dawn, and we spent a less than productive morning on the water. When I got back in early afternoon, Therese asked how the fishing was. "Not so good," I replied. "Well, did you and Bill have a good talk anyway?" "Naw, we didn't say much," I answered. She just looked at me for a minute. Finally, she asked incredulously, "Do you mean that the two of you sat next to one another for over four hours and didn't say anything?"

"Well, come to think of it," I replied, "Bill commented that it was a nice day and we did say 'Pass the worms' a couple of times."

Bill and I had a great time. Therese could only feel pity for two such warped personalities. Therese and Bill's wife, Barb, would have approached that fishing trip very differently.

Have you ever played cards or a board game with other couples? That setting is a good laboratory for observing this difference.

For a few years running, Therese and I would visit our friends Ken and Margie on New Year's afternoon to play bridge and then watch the Rose Bowl game. We rarely finished a rubber of bridge. Therese and Margie spent so much time and energy catching up on things, that it was impossible to keep card-play moving along fast enough to satisfy Ken and me. Ken and I would eventually give up and go watch whatever football game was on before the Rose Bowl.

What does this difference mean for us? It means that husbands need to be aware that their wives experience relationships through verbal communication to a greater degree than they do. One way for husbands to show their wives that they both love them and want to grow in their relationship is to initiate conversation more regularly and spontaneously than they might "naturally" be inclined.

Wives, on the other hand, should not expect from their husbands the same level of verbal interaction which they themselves would "naturally" be inclined to have and may, in fact, be used to in their relationships with other women. Wives need to have confidence that their husbands love them and feel close to them even though this gets communicated less verbally than they might wish.

Although these differences are God-given and should be respected, the effect of sin in our lives means that our differences don't always operate in the way God intends. Some men are not being verbal enough; some women talk too much. If so, the patterns need to change. We can't hide behind "That's just me." We can ask for and expect God's help so that we can move beyond our limitations to be better able to serve our spouse.

How to Have an Argument

Because we live an intimate and often intense life in marriage, we will have arguments from time to time. Arguments can sometimes creep up on you. You find yourselves arguing, and you cannot figure out how it happened. You can see other arguments coming from a long way off. Arguments can begin over many things:

Disagreement: "This room is too hot."—"No, it isn't, it's just right."

Misunderstanding: "I thought you were going to pick me up at noon."—"You said you wouldn't be ready till 1:30."

Unmet expectations: "I wanted this to be a nice, romantic time together, but you watched television the whole evening."

An unguarded word: "Meatloaf again?"

Arguments are not nice. More often than not they involve a good deal of unrighteous behavior: accusation, name-calling, threats, manipulation, silence, maybe even physical violence. They can leave a pall of hostility long after the action has stopped. Love is questioned and trust is broken. Even if some arguments are minor disagreements, they are nonetheless messy and unwelcome. They are surely not part of God's plan for marriage.

From the Christian perspective, the important thing is to handle arguments constructively. By dealing with arguments in the right way, we will not only make them less traumatic but actually turn them into something positive. Here is a plan we have developed over the years which will help you to reduce the number and intensity of arguments and, we hope, allow your relationship to emerge stronger from the arguments you do have.

Step 1: Talk about issues before they build up ("The best defense is a good offense"). We discussed this point earlier in the chapter, but it is worth repeating here. One of the great values of a regular communication time is that you and your spouse know that there is both a time to talk about problems and issues and a commitment on the part of both of you to actually talk about them. In most cases you should be able to bring the issue successfully to a common decision. Even when you can't, you are at least still working on it.

Step 2: If an argument begins, the partner who realizes first that things have gotten out of hand should immediately take steps to change things. This is a difficult step, and it requires discipline and cooperation to get it to work. But it is the surest way we know to short-circuit an argument. Here is an example of how it works.

John came home from working late for the third time this week. All three times he failed to call home to let Dorothy know, and supper turned cold long before he arrived. To top it all off, being late tonight not only ruined supper but ruined their plans to go out together this evening. Between six and eight o'clock, Dorothy had plenty of opportunity to build up a head of steam. When John finally walked in the door, she let him have both barrels. John, who didn't particularly like working late and was tired, immediately counterattacked and the war was on.

After about five minutes, Dorothy realized that they were having an argument. She called upon her inner reserves and the grace of God and said to John in a very different tone of voice than the one she had been using, "John, we shouldn't be doing this. I want to stop right now. I realize that I played a big part in getting us into it. I am angry, and I want to talk about your coming home late and not calling, but not like this. It was wrong for me to light into you the way I did. I'm sorry, will you forgive me?"

John takes a deep breath and says, "You are right. We shouldn't be acting like this. I want to stop too. I know I did my part to get us into it, and I was wrong too. Yes, I forgive you for the way you met me at the door. Will you forgive me for calling you an 'insensitive, nagging shrew'? It isn't what I really think about you, and I shouldn't have said it."

Dorothy: "Yes, I forgive you."

John: "I know we need to discuss this further. I want to. I know I should have called."

Dorothy: "Let me scrape your supper off the wall so you can eat."

John: "O.K. Let's talk about the problem as soon as the kitchen is cleaned."

This argument, like many, had the potential to continue a long time. The key to ending it was Dorothy's realization of what was happening and deciding to not allow the sinful pattern to continue. John had an important role as well—he had to choose to follow Dorothy's lead in the matter. If he hadn't, the argument would have continued.

Dorothy and John were not simply applying a technique, but were applying the scriptural pattern for how Christians should relate to one another.

They recognized and admitted to wrongdoing (sin). "Let no evil talk come out of your mouths, but only such as is good for edifying, as fits the occasion, that you may impart grace to those who hear. And do not grieve the Holy Spirit of God, in whom you were sealed for the day of redemption. Let all bitterness and wrath and anger and clamor and slander be put away from you with all malice" (Eph 4:29-31).

They confessed their wrongdoing and sought forgiveness. "Therefore confess your sins to one another, and pray for one another, that you may be healed" (Jas 5:16).

They forgave one another. "Then Peter came up and said to him, 'Lord, how often shall my brother sin against me, and I forgive him? As many as seven times?' Jesus said to him, 'I do not say to you seven times, but seventy times seven'" (Mt 18:21-22).

"And be kind to one another, tenderhearted, forgiving one another, as God in Christ forgave you" (Eph 4:32).

They desired peace and unity above their own hurt. "I therefore, a prisoner for the Lord, beg you to lead a life worthy of the calling to which you have been called, with all lowliness and meekness, with patience, forbearing one another in love, eager to maintain the unity of the Spirit in the bond of peace" (Eph 4:1-2).

We want to emphasize the scriptural pattern for two reasons. The first we have already stated: husband and wife are brother and sister in the Lord and should treat one another as such. Secondly, we follow the scriptural pattern because this is God's pattern for our relationship. We can trust that his grace will be present to us to enable us to follow through once we begin.

Trying to employ this step as merely a human technique won't work. There is no human motivation to make it work. It's easier to blow off steam and say whatever comes to mind—to try and "win" the argument. Besides, without the power of the Holy Spirit, a couple only has its own human strength to break the pattern, and simple human strength just isn't enough.

Step 3: After you regain control of the situation, evaluate what happened.

Discuss the dynamics. What caused each person to react wrongly?

"When you went silent on me, all I could think of to get you to respond was to throw the magazine at you." "When you accused me, I got defensive."

The point is not to excuse ourselves for wrongdoing or to blame the other person, but to recognize the effect our actions or words have on the other person so that we can avoid problems in the future.

Make agreements about changes. For example, agree to not walk out, to not remain silent, to not throw things, to not bring up the past, to be more eager to repent.

Make sure that adequate reconciliation has taken place. Are there any words or actions for which either of you still need to repent? Be sure to do so because it clears the air and doesn't give resentment a foothold.

Step 4: Discuss the issue that began the argument if there is one. The reason for this step should be obvious. If you really don't have time to resolve the issue immediately, at least decide specifically when you will discuss it.

Step 5: Pray together. Bring what has just happened to the Lord together. Ask him to restore peace and harmony to your relationship, and to protect you from bitterness or self-pity or lack of true forgiveness. Pray for the issue that began it. Ask him to give you wisdom and unity on the matter.

Step 6: Express affection. Some expression of physical affection helps dispel whatever residual feelings of distance or coldness you experienced during the argument. After you have brought your argument through the above steps, we highly recommend that you break through that last barrier of internal resistance so that anger, self-pity, and self-righteousness are effectively buried. After an argument, the last thing you want to do is touch your spouse. You go out of your way to avoid one another. If you go to bed feeling that way, you move as far to "your own side" of the bed as possible. Double beds sure seem small at a time like that.

Don't let it happen. An embrace or a kiss or holding hands for a few moments is a very fitting and effective way to break through that last barrier and restore your relationship.

To Do This Week

Individual Time

Answer the questions:
1. Did I pray for my spouse and our marriage this week?

2. How do I think our communication time was this week?

3. How do I rate myself on the dos and don'ts of good communication?

Dos	*Often*	*Sometimes*	*Almost never*
Straightforward and clear	———	———	———
Patient	———	———	———
Attentive	———	———	———
Try to understand spouse	———	———	———
Acknowledge perception difference	———	———	———
Accept responsibility for wrongdoing and ask forgiveness	———	———	———

Don'ts	*Often*	*Sometimes*	*Almost never*
Dump	———	———	———
Be defensive	———	———	———
Need an answer	———	———	———
Use "always," "never"	———	———	———
Call into question spouse's love and commitment	———	———	———
Force spouse to deal with something right away	———	———	———
Have to be right	———	———	———
Use sarcasm	———	———	———
Bring up the past	———	———	———
Interrupt	———	———	———
Walk out	———	———	———

Use silent treatment	___	___	___
Use emotional manipulation	___	___	___
Use nonverbal interruptions	___	___	___

4. Pick out your two worst dos and your three worst don'ts and decide how to change them.

5. Pick out the two things your spouse does wrong from the above lists which you would most like to see change.

Time Together

1. Share your answers to the questions above.

2. Review the steps for having a successful argument.

—If you can remember your last argument (it may have occurred while sharing your answers to #5 above) use Step 3 and evaluate it.

3. Commit yourselves to following the guidelines for a successful argument.

4. Pray that God will help you both make the changes you need in how you speak to one another.

For further reading:

H. Norman Wright, *Communication: Key to Your Marriage* (Glendale, Calif.: Regal Books, 1974).

God's Peace Plan: Love

YOU MAY BE ASKING yourselves, "How can the two of *us*, with all of our faults and shortcomings, live the ideal presented in the first chapter?" Fortunately for us, our Creator knows his creatures. He knows both his creatures and his ideal for marriage and has given us what we call God's "peace plan."

God's peace plan has two parts—*both* parts are essential to make the whole thing work. *Agape-love* and *order in marriage* (next chapter) are the two essentials that enable people like us to live the kind of life that God intends for all of his people. This chapter and the one following are designed to work in tandem.

God's Love—Our Love

Love is an over-used word. We "fall in love"; he "loves" baseball; I "love" chocolate; I "love" my husband; and I "love" my new tennis racket. All express different ranges of emotion and meaning, and all use the same word. So, when we begin to speak about Christian marriage and the love that a husband and a wife should have for each other, the word "love" can be rather threadbare.

In the New Testament the word "love" translates four different Greek words. Only two concern us in our discussion of married love—*eros,* the physical attraction experienced between men and women (erotic love) and *agape,* the love that God has for us and the type of love that we are exhorted to have for one another.

> That you, being rooted and grounded in love, may have power to comprehend with all the saints what is the breadth and length and height and depth, and to know the love of Christ which surpasses knowledge, that you may be filled with all the fulness of God.
>
> (Eph 3:17-19)

Most people's understanding of married love is the romantic one—*eros.* Some couples, in an attempt to "put the love back" in their marriages, try to recreate dating patterns that are designed to stir memories and exciting romantic feelings of being "in love." Many marriage help books and programs emphasize efforts to recreate that "falling in love" feeling of the early years.

There is nothing wrong with those exciting days when you jumped every time the phone rang and felt knots in the pit of your stomach when the door bell rang. But it just isn't enough to make a marriage work. Attraction, sex, and spring flowers don't hold up under the pressure of conflict and stress. Personal attraction is too fragile and fleeting to have something as important as lifelong fidelity resting on it. Attraction can come, but it goes just as quickly.

The Key to a Better Marriage

"Therefore, be *imitators* of God as beloved children. And walk in love, as Christ loved us and gave himself up for us, a fragrant offering and sacrifice to God" (Eph 5:1-2).

We believe that if both partners make a commitment to apply the scriptural agape *meaning of love toward each other, marriage will flourish! Your marriage will be marked with a unity, peace, and power that is impossible through human effort or attraction.*

The great scholar William Barclay describes the meaning of the word *agape* in this way: "Agape has to do with the mind; it is not simply an emotion which rises unbidden in our hearts; it is a principle by which we deliberately live. Agape has supremely to do with the will. It is a conquest, a victory, an achievement. . . . it is the power to love the unlovable, to love people whom we do not like."

Barclay goes on: *Agape,* he says, "is the love that God has for us and the love that God invites us to have through the power of the Holy Spirit. No matter what a man is like, God seeks nothing but his highest good."

For the Christian couple it is critical to realize that their marriage should be based on *agape* love, a love that operates independently of *attraction, emotions,* and *circumstances.* So when circumstances (family, age, finances) change, their loving behavior does not. When physical attraction decreases, their loving commitment will not weaken.

Why? Because of the very definition of *agape* love itself: *Agape* has to do with the mind; it is not simply an emotion which rises unbidden in our hearts; it is a *principle* to live by.

The key to a satisfying, rich, and fruitful marriage is that its foundation be the kind of love that God has for us—not physical attraction and mutual compatibility. The marriage relationship is often the one place that Christians fail to apply the very basics of Christian relating. Throughout the New Testament, Christians are encouraged, exhorted, and commanded to relate to one another in godly love. It is often in those relationships closest to us that it is the hardest to love as Christ loves. The marriage relationship can be the easiest place to sin by being unkind and uncharitable in speech and in our actions. If we base our relationship on the principles explained in scripture and act in Christian love, many "marriage problems" will never arise. Most of the problems in marriages are the result of sin—sin in thoughts, sin in actions, and sin in speech.

Be Practical!

Does this principle of *agape* love sound too vague for you? Let's be practical. Let's begin to put scripture in action in our lives with the classic verses on love in the New Testament.

Love is patient and kind; love is not jealous or boastful; it is not arrogant or rude. Love does not insist on its own way; it is not irritable or resentful; it does not rejoice at wrong but rejoices in the right. Love bears all things, believes all things, hopes all things, endures all things. (1 Cor 13:4-7)

Imagine applying the "Love is patient" principle to your daily life. Most of us could name certain areas of our spouse's personal life that either *should* change, or areas that we would *like* to see changed, usually for our own convenience.

Some of these desired changes may have to do with money. Joyce, a friend of ours, constantly forgot to enter the amount of a check that she had written or to check the balance of the checkbook before she wrote another check. Frank, Joyce's husband, was not only irritated at her poor money managing; he was alarmed. The family was on a tight budget, and accurate accounting was crucial for their finances.

Over the years Joyce's laxness in accounting had been the source of much tension in the marriage. They would argue. Frank would often shout at his wife and say things about her character that he regretted. It often took days to undo the damage done by these conflicts.

Joyce got some help and was making slow progress in handling money. Frank knew he should support her determined efforts to change, but he got angry every time she did forget. Then he read the verses in Corinthians: "love is patient," and "there is no limit to love's forbearance." He decided to apply this teaching by being patient and forbearing rather than righteously angry every time Joyce failed.

Frank's decision had a very positive effect on their whole marriage. Instead of money being the root of anger for him and a source of depression for Joyce, Frank's patience and forbearance gave Joyce the freedom and encouragement she needed to grow in this area that she was so weak in. Let's take another verse in 1 Corinthians 13. "Love does not insist on its own way."

Sometimes our schedules can be so hectic that if I (Therese) am busy one day, dinner can be a *very* informal affair: "Do you want leftover sloppy-joes or a tuna sandwich?" One day, after a particularly long run on informal dinners, I was beginning to feel that I wasn't serving Randy as well as I should be and that I should make dinner a little more special. It was another one of "those" days. Between a run to the orthodontist with our teenage son and picking up the next batch of kids after school and before a meeting I couldn't skip, I tried to throw together a nice dinner. No matter what happened, Randy was going to be loved by me by having a special dinner.

Randy found me on the kitchen floor with my head in the bottom cupboard, cookbooks spread all over the counters, and the microwave dutifully trying to defrost a hunk of frozen hamburger meat. The baby was methodically smashing saltines on the floor under the table, and our three-year-old was taking great joy in handing her more to demolish.

Tentatively he asked, "What are you doing?" With a determined look on my face, I said, "I'm trying to match a recipe with what I have on hand in the house so I won't have to go to the store." "Well," Randy said, "I just came in to tell you not to cook anything for dinner tonight because you've had such a hectic week and today is pretty crazy for you. Burgers out tonight is my treat."

"But I wanted to do something special for *you* because you've been so good about putting up with dinners this week."

Well, we wound up out at the local burger place. But no matter what actually happened that night for dinner, our love and mutual respect was built because neither of us approached the situation with a self-serving attitude. I could have demanded to be taken out because I was over-extended, or Randy could have gone around feeling sorry for himself. Instead, as the years go on, we naturally think more and more about how we can serve one another.

Imagine if every marriage was ruled by 1 Corinthians 13! Many marriage problems can be worked out in the normal course of the day as we look to scripture as a very real guide for our daily life.

A Show Stopper

Let's look at another simple verse that we're all familiar with. Matthew 7:12 says, "So whatever you wish that men would do to you, do so to them; for this is the law and the prophets."

Any time I'm tempted to give in to a petty spirit of being angry because I feel I have the "right" to be angry, I stop, and the words go through my mind: "Do unto others . . . ."

One evening I very accurately and eloquently showed Randy how I thought something he had done had not been right. (Isn't it amazing how some things seem so important at the time and later we can't even remember what the specifics were?) He thought for a long time and agreed that I was right. Later, however, Randy pointed out something to me. He said that if he had corrected *me* on a similar point, I would have asked him to be more patient and understanding. He thought I used a double standard sometimes. "You want me to understand *you*, but you expect perfection from me," he said.

I could see that he was right. I did expect close to perfection from my husband, but I expected Randy to be always loving, patient, and kind with *me* when I did something wrong!

Isn't this true of all of us? Before we jump to speak any correction, remember the verse from Matthew, "Do unto others . . . ." This verse can lead to more love and kindness in our marriages than any human sense of personal justice and verbal persuasion.

Spirit Powered

Agape love has to make a difference in the overall quality of the marriage relationship. Christian love is other-centered not self-centered. When *agape* love is actually applied to a marriage, the consequences are *dramatic*. But humanly speaking, these results are impossible. The most natural tendency for all of us is to think about how things affect *me*. How will this decision affect me and the things that I think are important?

We can live the high ideal of *agape* love only in the power of the Holy Spirit. Christianity is made that way. It is impossible to live the Christian life without the power of God's Holy Spirit. It is critical for husbands and wives to acknowledge to themselves, to each other, and to the Lord that without him we can do nothing.

Also, it is impossible to love as God loves without *knowing* the love of God himself. We need to search in scripture and turn to God in prayer so that we may know God's love more fully, so that *we* can love as God loves.

By Their Fruit You Shall Know Them

The Lord blesses our efforts to follow him. While we surrender our lives and wills to Jesus, God gives us peace, unity, and joy. As we exercise *agape* love, we are blessed with *philia* love—"affectionate regard, warm feelings and depth of relationship."

As we seek after God and the things of God, our marriages and families will bear the mark of his presence. "Seek ye first the kingdom of God and all else will be given to you" (Lk 12:31).

To better understand what a Christian marriage is like, let us compare it to a secular marriage based on human effort and mutual enjoyment.

> I therefore, a prisoner for the Lord, beg you to lead a life worthy of the calling to which you have been called, with all lowliness and meekness, with patience, forbearing one another in love, eager to maintain the unity of the spirit in the bond of peace. (Eph 4:1-3)

How Christian and Secular Marriages Should Be Different

Area of Life	Christian	Secular
individual	is committed to Jesus Christ	is committed to self-fulfillment—personal rights
couple	marriage is centered on Jesus	is centered on personal happiness
goal	unity—one mind, one heart, one life	individual satisfaction, success
power	from the Holy Spirit	personal motivation, personality strength
marriage vows	life commitment, sexual fidelity, loyalty	as long as it is working, to become a "full person"
love	*Agape* love rules; erotic does not rule	erotic love, attraction, circumstances, and feelings rule
ideal	the family dedicated to know, love, serve God	personal happiness
children	as an integral part of the union, whether natural, or foster, or adopted	none or few, at convenience of career or personal pleasure
home	a place of refreshment for family and others, a place from which to serve others	a refuge from the world and responsibilities

Area of Life	Christian	Secular
end result	unity, peace, joy in serving Christ and His kingdom	usually self-centered; high divorce rate, partially or non-satisfying

To Do This Week

Individual Time

Answer the questions:

1. Have I prayed for my spouse and our marriage this week?

2. Before reading this chapter, what did you mean when you said, "I love you" to your spouse?
   Example: When I say "I love you" I mean
   I am very fond of you
   I am sexually attracted to you
   I am committed to you
   I want the best for you
   Etc.

3. Has the concept of *agape* love caused you to revise or expand this list? If so, make a new one.
   Read 1 Corinthians 13 again. Pick out the three specific expressions of love you think your spouse does best with.
   Example:
   patience: because of how she is with children

Now pick out the three specific expressions of love you think *you* have the biggest problem doing. What concretely can you do to change?

Time Together

1. Share your answers from your individual activity.

2. Pray together that *agape* love rule and empower your marriage. Here are some other scriptures to reflect on:

Matthew 18:21-22—Forgiveness
John 13:13-17—Washing the feet of the apostles
John 13:34—Love one another
Romans 12:9-21—Christian behavior
Romans 13:9-10—Love fulfills the law
Galatians 5:13-15—Love means service
Ephesians 5:22-33—God's order in marriage

For further reading:

C.S. Lewis, *The Four Loves* (New York: Harcourt Brace Jovanovich, 1960).

Week Five

God's Peace Plan: Order

T HE SECOND KEY ELEMENT in God's peace plan for marriage is how the husband-wife relationship is ordered. Every set of human relationships needs a structure in order to function well. Whenever people join together to work toward a common goal—erecting a skyscraper, climbing a mountain, setting up a neighborhood concerns committee, or launching a marriage—they need agreed-upon ways of relating together. Otherwise the job will never get finished and the group will fall apart in chaos and disunity.

The marriage relationship is the most basic way people join together for a common goal. Because God is so invested in marriages working well, he has provided the pattern for how the husband and wife should work together. The pattern is found in scripture. To foster peace and unity in the marriage relationship, God has structured it so that husband and wife work together as a team with the husband as the head of the team and the wife subordinate to him. Ephesians 5:22-33 provides us with one of the clearest statements in scripture of God's plan for order within marriage. Paul writes:

Wives, be subject to your husbands, as to the Lord. For the husband is the head of the wife as Christ is the head of the church, his body, and is himself its Savior. As the church is subject to Christ, so let wives also be subject in everything to their husbands. Husbands, love your wives, as Christ loved the church and gave himself up for her, that he might sanctify her, having cleansed her by the washing of water with the word, that he might present the church to himself in splendor, without spot or wrinkle or any such thing, that she might be holy and without blemish. Even so husbands should love their wives as their own bodies. He who loves his wife loves himself. For no man ever hates his own flesh, but nourishes and cherishes it, as Christ does the church, because we are members of his body. "For this reason a man shall leave his father and mother and be joined to his wife, and the two shall become one flesh." This mystery is a profound one, and I am saying that it refers to Christ and the church; however, let each one of you love his wife as himself, and let the wife see that she respects her husband.

God's plan calls for the husband to be the head of his wife (as Christ) and for the wife to be submissive to her husband (as the church). It is a simple plan. Living it brings joy, peace, and unity to the marriage.

However, some people have a negative reaction to the principle of headship and submission in marriage. They dismiss the idea as unrealistic or unworkable. Some of the reasons for negative reactions are legitimate and should be acknowledged. Other objections have little objective merit but must be confronted nonetheless. Here are some of the more common objections to headship and submission we have encountered over the years.

1. *The reality of male sexism. Some men do oppress women out of either fear, insecurity, ego-needs, upbringing, or other reasons.*

One couple we know had a substantial problem in this area. Peter, the husband, controlled everything from money to how the house should look. He gave Karen, his wife, very little money to buy food, but always complained that there wasn't enough for dinner. Karen received no personal spending money, but Peter always had enough money to buy whatever he needed. Peter often complained about how the home looked, sometimes in the presence of the children and guests, but he never gave her any help. Peter had a general disdain for women, and he regularly focused it on Karen. Understandably, Karen rejected any discussion about the husband's headship over the marriage.

2. *Some men don't love, respect, and care for their wives.*

Some men fail to show their wives that they care for them. While they don't actually "oppress" their wives, these husbands are inconsiderate of their wives' needs and basically leave them to fend for themselves. It's very difficult to ask a wife to submit to her husband when she isn't really sure of his basic love for her.

3. *Some wives don't respect their husbands.*

When a wife has a general disdain for her husband's ideas, directions, or ways of doing things, it's hard for him to get excited about leading the family. He doesn't know if she is going to be with him on it or not.

4. *Some wives don't want anyone "over" them.*

Many people think that being subordinate to someone else means that you are either inferior or incompetent. Wives who believe this false idea will find it difficult to put themselves into such a position.

5. *Fear of authority.*

Both men and women often fear authority because it can be abused. In marriage, some wives are afraid of being under authority and some husbands are afraid to exercise it.

6. *Some husbands don't want anyone "under" them.*

Some men simply don't want to accept the responsibility that comes with headship. They are content to let things happen or to let their wives lead because that's easier. They can just drift.

7. *Confusion between submission and passivity.*

A common misunderstanding about headship and submission is that being submissive means being passive. People don't want to submit because they think it means not doing anything until you are told and not exercising any initiative or creativity.

8. *The belief that scriptural directions about headship and submission are cultural and relate to the social situation of the world of the writer.*

This notion has gained great popularity among Christians in the last twenty years. We have an entirely different culture now, at least in the West, runs the argument. And since these scripture passages come from a culture that no longer exists, we are not bound by them.

Two passages in scripture clearly refute this objection.

In 1 Corinthians 11:3, Paul relates headship and submission between a husband and wife not to the culture of his time or any previous time, nor to his own opinion, but to the order within the Godhead. In Ephesians 5:22-24, Paul relates the husband-wife relationship in marriage to the transcultural relationship between Christ and the church.

For a more complete discussion of the normative nature of headship and submission in marriage, we recommend *Man and Woman in Christ* by Stephen B. Clark (Ann Arbor: Servant Publications, 1980).

In light of these negative reactions to God's order in marriage, how should we approach it? How can husbands and wives overcome these obstacles and relate in the right way? There are two great principles which put the relationship between husband and wife, especially headship and submission, in the right perspective: the Galatians principle and the Ephesians principle.

The Galatians Principle

Husband and wife are son and daughter of God, brother and sister in the Lord. Paul writes: "But when the time had fully come, God sent forth his Son, born of woman, born under the law, to redeem those who were under the law so that we might receive adoption as sons. And because you are sons [and daughters], God has sent the spirit of his Son into our hearts crying, 'Abba! Father.' So through God you are no longer a slave but a son, and if a son then an heir" (Gal 4:4-7).

Do you realize, husband, that you married God's daughter? Do you realize, wife, that you married God's son? Granted, your spouse may not always act as a son or daughter of God should, but that doesn't change the facts. That person you married was redeemed by Christ's blood and adopted by the Father. Your spouse has an inherent dignity and worth because of his or her standing before God. You need to give your spouse the honor, esteem, and dignity due them.

We vividly remember the first time we encountered this profound idea.

On Valentine's Day, 1970, we were among several Christian couples invited to a friend's home to consume a pink frosted heart-shaped cake in a candle-lit living room. The setting evoked romantic sentiments. We were all young married couples still in the first flush of romantic love.

Also present was a Christian pastor visiting from out of town. He had been married for about twenty years. Since he knew a good deal about marriage, we asked him to say a few things that would inspire young couples. We were all expecting him to make remarks that would fit the mood of the evening. However, what he said was about as jarring as if someone had turned on a giant floodlight in the little room.

The pastor looked around at us and said, "You know, being husband and wife is not the most important fact of your marriage relationship. What is even more important and basic is the fact that you are brother and sister in the Lord." The mood in the room changed immediately. Who wants to be married to a brother or sister? we thought.

Everyone in the room was smiling politely, but not enthusiastically, as the thought sank in. The pastor explained: "Because each one of you has been brought into a relationship with Jesus, you have been given the same spirit of sonship which he has. You are God's sons and daughters. Hence, in a real sense, you are brothers and sisters. That means you have to treat one another the way scripture says brothers and sisters of Christ should. You can't make allowances or excuses for yourselves. The great temptation in marriage is to begin taking one another for granted. After you have lived together for some years, and you have seen each other's faults and imperfections, you become less considerate of your spouse and perhaps begin disliking many of the things your spouse does. You can become critical and negative and fail to show your spouse the proper esteem and respect. Worst of all, husbands and wives can become blind to the fact that the standards of speech, forgiveness, and service that scripture sets for how Christians should relate to one another apply to married partners as well. The closeness and exclusiveness of the marriage relationship does not mean married people have a different set of standards. If you were to see one another as God sees you, you would experience a revolution in your marriage."

We talked about this after we got home that evening, and we also talked to some of our friends later. We agreed that the pastor was right, and we needed to have the perspective he described. We made a commitment to have this truth—that we are first of all brothers and sisters in the Lord—form the basis of our life together in marriage. It has made a tremendous difference over the past fifteen years. When we get tempted to be lazy or neglectful or sinful in our relationship with each other, we remind ourselves that this is God's son or daughter I'm dealing with, and that I had better have a good reason (one our Father will accept) for acting the way I am. Think about that the next time you get ready to treat your spouse in a way you shouldn't. It will stop you cold.

The Ephesians Principle

The marriage relationship is like the relationship between Christ and the church. Just as Christ and the church are intimately bound together and form a unity, so are husband and wife. The order within marriage should mirror the order between Christ and the church. Christ, the head of the church, loves and serves the church; the church, submitted to Christ, respects, loves, and serves Christ. As Christ and the church love and serve one another, so should husband and wife.

The ideal for the husband's relationship with his wife is Christ's relationship with his church. Husbands, read through that passage in Ephesians again and reflect on what it says about how you should be the head of your wife. You can use the chart below to help you focus your thoughts.

Christ	**Husband**
Died for the church to save it	Am I willing to give up (die to) my personal needs and desires for the good of my wife? There is no room here for "oppression" or "macho" ideals. The path of Christ is death to self.
Christ makes the church holy	Am I willing to do whatever is necessary for my wife to be a strong, holy woman of God?
Christ loves the church as himself	Do I love my wife as I do myself? Am I as concerned about her as I am about myself?
Christ and the church are one	Do I think of my wife as a part of me, or is she just "the woman I live with who is useful for

some things, but just in the way at other times"? Do I consult with her to get her input and ideas for our life together?

Gives the church direction and guidance	Am I willing to take responsibility for my wife, our life together, and our children by setting directions and making decisions even if they are unpopular?

The ideal for the wife's relationship with her husband is found in the church's relationship to Christ. Wives, read through that passage in Ephesians again and reflect on what it says about how you should be submitted to your husband. Here is a chart to help you focus your thoughts.

Church	Wife
Subject to the Lord	Do I see submission to my husband as a way of submitting to the Lord? Am I, in fact, submitted to the Lord in my life?
Subject in everything	Am I willing to let my husband into every area of my life for his care? Am I willing to trust him and let him make mistakes? Do I try to manipulate him to do what I want?
Respects Christ	Do I respect my husband? Do I respect his way of doing things? Do I respect him simply because he is my husband even though he has not earned my respect by being perfect?
The church is one with Christ	Am I one with my husband? Do I want to know his mind on things? Is he part of me or the man I have to live around?

Both husband and wife will need to work to bring God's order to marriage. Both should make a verbal commitment to live by the principles of Galatians 4:4-7 and Ephesians 5:22-33. Even if you have been doing things out of God's order for years, it's not too late to make a new beginning. Because it's God's life you want to live, he will give you power to live differently.

Headship and submission are not an ends in themselves. Our ultimate goal is life with God. Our immediate goal is a marriage marked by strength, unity, and peace. The proper order between husband and wife who understand themselves as brother and sister in the Lord is one of the keys to reaching our immediate goal. Headship and submission have to be part of our overall life. They can't grow without love and respect. Without love and respect, headship and submission become legalistic and will not produce the fruit they promise.

In the next two weeks we are going to look at how husbands and wives can concretely put into practice the principles of love and order we have discussed in these last two weeks.

To Do This Week

Individual Time

Answer the questions:
1. Did I pray for my spouse and our marriage this week?

2. Did I adequately prepare for our communication time this week?

3. What are the two most helpful things I personally received from this chapter? Why were they so helpful?

4. (Husbands) Go back to pages 64-65 and honestly answer the questions we suggested for the husband.

5. (Husbands) What is the one area of submission we listed for wives you would most like to see change in your wife—your sister in the Lord?

6. (Wives) Go back to page 65 and honestly answer the questions we posed for the wife.

7. (Wives) What is the one area of headship we listed for husbands you would most like to see change in your husband—your brother in the Lord?

Time Together

1. Share with one another your answers to the above questions.

2. Talk about how you can bring God's order more into your marriage.

3. Make a commitment to do it.

For further reading:

Jay Adams, *Christian Living in the Home* (Grand Rapids: Baker Book House, 1972), chapters 6 and 7.

Week Six

At Your Service: How Husbands Care for Their Wives

A S WE SAW IN THE LAST CHAPTER, the husband's role of headship is a role of service and love. It is not a self-serving position where the husband "lords it over" his wife. Rather, it is the same position of service that Christ took in relation to the church. Scripture, in fact, admonishes all Christians who are in headship or leadership roles to have the Lord's attitude toward their position.

> A dispute also arose among them, which of them was to be regarded as the greatest. And he [Jesus] said to them, "The kings of the Gentiles exercise lordship over them; and those in authority over them are called benefactors. But not so with you; rather let the greatest among you become as the youngest, and the leader as one who serves. For which is the greater, one who sits at table or one who serves? Is it not the one who sits at table? But I am among you as one who serves."
>
> (Lk 22:24-27)

Jesus tells his disciples that we can't look to the world to understand God's ways. We especially have to get God's mind about authority and power if we are going to avoid abusing them. Jesus points to his own life as an example of how to exercise authority and commands his followers to do likewise.

> When he had washed their feet and taken his garments, and resumed his place, he said to them, "Do you know what I have done to you? You call me Teacher and Lord; and you are right, for so I am. If I then, your Lord and Teacher, have washed your feet, you also ought to wash one another's feet. For I have given you an example, that you also should do as I have done to you." (Jn 13:12-15)

Jesus doesn't deny that he is greater than the disciples. In fact, he readily admits he is Teacher and Lord. He then points out that if he, who is greater than any of them, can serve them by performing a task (foot-washing) reserved for slaves, how much more should they, who are all brothers, serve one another's needs.

> Do nothing from selfishness or conceit, but in humility count others better than yourselves. Let each of you look not only to his own interests but also to the interests of others. Have this mind among yourselves, which is yours in Christ Jesus, who, though he was in the form of God, did not count equality with God a thing to be grasped, but emptied himself taking the form of a servant, being born in the likeness of men. (Phil 2:3-7)

Here again, scripture tells Christians to put others first by serving them. And again we find Jesus being held as the model for how to think and act.

While none of the above passages mentions marriage specifically, the application to marriage is clear and unmistakable: husband and wife should relate to one another as Christ relates to us. However, since we are only concerned about husbands in this chapter, I would like the husbands to try a little exercise. Go back over these three scripture passages and think about how they specifically apply to you in your role as husband. Do you "lord it over" your wife? Do you seek to be served rather than to serve? Do you "wash your wife's feet"—that is, do you refresh her? Do you look out for yourself and leave your wife to take care of herself? Is Jesus the model for how you relate to your wife? Or are Clint Eastwood's movie roles? Do you see your wife as worthy of your service? She is.

The pattern we find in scripture for how husbands should relate to their wives doesn't have any room for oppressive overbearing actions or selfish motives. Scripture rules out all macho behavior. Husbands are not to treat wives as inferior or as objects the husband can relate to when and how he pleases. Rather, scripture teaches a husband that, as the head of his wife, he has a command from God to follow the example of Christ and see himself as his wife's servant. Difficult? You bet. Impossible? No. Living the ideal begins with a basic attitude change, so that our minds and hearts conform to God's. Husbands can ask God's help to change the attitudes or habits that may have been working for years.

Along with the attitude change, there are some immediate concrete ways husbands can begin exercising headship service in their marriage. I (Randy) want to present here a very practical list of ways that a husband can care for his wife in the way that God wants.

1. *Pray for her.* I take time regularly during my personal prayer to bring my wife before the Lord. I pray that God will bless her with every good gift; that he will draw her closer to himself; that he will take care of whatever needs she may have. I pray against whatever trials or difficulties she may be experiencing, and I ask God to give me wisdom for how to serve her. I believe that the most important way a husband can serve his wife is to bring her deeper into the Lord's life. What better way to do it than through prayer? Prayer is not the only way a husband can lead his wife closer to the Lord, but it is the one way *every* husband can commit himself to. A husband may not know much scripture or theology, and he may not have a good pastoral sense of what needs to happen for his wife. But he can pray. Prayer is powerful. It changes things. It brings husbands right to the seat of grace and wisdom—God himself.

As I pray for Therese regularly, I become more aware of the areas of our life together where something needs to happen. One day during prayer, for example, I concluded that Therese and I should talk about how our three oldest children were doing. The next morning, I told her I thought we should talk about Tim, Tom, and Jenny. Therese said she had been wanting to do that for some time, but hadn't brought it up because we had been so busy. That's a small, but typical example of how the Lord can intervene in our marriage if we are faithful to prayer. That conversation was very good for both of us, and it put Therese's mind at ease about a couple of areas of concern she had for our oldest kids.

If there is any one thing I would tell husbands about wives, it's *pray for them.*

2. *Communication.* The husband should take responsibility to see that adequate regular communication is taking place. Even though you may have agreed together with your wife about when and where to talk about things, you should be aggressive about getting it to happen.

One couple I know had agreed to have a regular communication time every week. For a few weeks they actually met together and were enthusiastic about it. Eventually, the husband lost his enthusiasm and began waiting for his wife to remind him about it—which eventually turned into nagging about it. Finally, the communication time just petered out.

Most husbands have a natural inclination to let communication fall to the lowest level their wives are willing to put up with. Being a good head means fighting that temptation and making sure that full, rich communication takes place.

The husband should also see to it that the right things are being discussed. He shouldn't sit around waiting to see what his wife wants to "talk about this time." If you don't know what to talk about, go back to chapter two and reread it.

Communication is a key area of married life. It should be an opportunity for the husband to lead the marriage and family by seeing to it that things are talked about which will build up and strengthen the marriage.

3. *Oversee her schedule.* One great service a husband performs is to help his wife set up a workable schedule for her day and week. This does not mean that wives are incapable of taking responsibility for their day. The point is that we all need to have some sort of objective, outside input on how we are setting priorities and scheduling the things which must get done. (Every husband should find another trusted, committed Christian man to provide this same objective review of his schedule.)

If your wife has difficulty organizing and sorting out priorities, you will have to spend more time each week working on her schedule. On the other hand, if your wife is well organized and astute about priorities, once her basic schedule is set, you shouldn't need to spend much time going over things.

If *you* have a problem with organization and priorities, get help, either from someone you know who is good at such things or from a book on the subject.

Some men are married to women who are better organized than they are. If you are in this category, chances are you have a problem which needs to be overcome in order for you to be an effective leader for the family. Get help.

You should keep in mind that, no matter how organized your wife might be, the changing circumstances at home will greatly affect her ability to "follow a schedule." Young children, sick family members, and other demands can make it difficult to maintain a routine, so patience and understanding on your part are essential. On the other hand, if your wife allows things to disrupt her schedule needlessly, you should help her overcome this problem.

You should take particular care to see that your wife has adequate time during each week for prayer and scripture reading. It may be impossible to find time every day, but you should try. She should at least be able to pray three or four times a week. You may need to take care of the children or do a chore or two for your wife so that she has the time. You may even have to give up something you want to do to give her time with the Lord. It's worth it. You should be as concerned for your wife's spiritual life as you are for your own.

Having a workable schedule can bring a lot of peace and order to your wife's life. Also, I think we have all experienced that when our wives' lives are peaceful and ordered, the atmosphere in the home reflects it. So by taking concern for your wife's schedule, you can have a large impact on the tenor of the home as well.

4. *Make decisions and give directions (both popular and unpopular).* Christian leadership is not at all like the authoritarian stereotype of the boss: giving orders and making decisions for others to carry out. However, Christian leadership in marriage does involve making decisions and giving directions. At times we will find that we have reached an impasse in a discussion about an issue, and a decision needs to be made. In general, the husband then needs to make the decision, and the wife should submit to it with a willing spirit.

Larry and Jane were having a difficult time making ends meet financially. Larry was in a low-paying dead-end job and was unable to find another, better-paying job. Larry wanted Jane to go to work for a while to help out financially. Since their children were all in school, he didn't see an important need for Jane to be in the home all day. Jane disagreed. She wasn't all that opposed to working; she just didn't think she could leave the home for the whole day, five days a week. Even though all the children were at school, Jane thought her full-time presence at home was important. She was willing to do even greater belt-tightening to help make ends meet. Larry thought that further belt-tightening was unrealistic since they were already living on the edge of their finances.

Larry and Jane went around and around on the issue for weeks without getting any closer to a common decision. Finally, with the beginning of school at hand and all the usual school expenses for the children piling up, Larry decided that action was needed. A good job had become available for Jane, and Larry said he wanted her to take it. Jane did. Jane hadn't changed her mind about wanting to stay at home, but she decided to do what Larry asked her to do. After a couple of months of working, Jane realized that she was still able to care for the life of the home without undue stress. This considerably relieved the tension she initially experienced about going to work. In addition, she saw how the added income alleviated the great financial strain the family was experiencing. She was eventually able to see that Larry had made the right decision, and she was glad he stuck to it despite her reluctance.

We know other husbands and wives for whom the decision to have the wife *not* work is the impasse. In ever-increasing numbers today, wives and mothers are returning to work in order to ease the financial strain on the family. In some cases, such as Larry and Jane, that was the direction Larry (and eventually Jane) deemed best. In other cases, however, the financial question may need to take a back seat to the greater good of having the mother remain at home and care for the children and the home.

A brief aside: the world today places little or no value on the role of motherhood in its traditional sense—a married woman remaining at home providing the primary care for the children and making the home a place of joy, refreshment, and service. Because of this "loss of value" and the financial burdens of raising a family, many Christian couples are automatically opting to have the wife work. We don't believe the "working mother" is a foregone conclusion for Christian families today. We urge each couple to seek God's guidance for their own situation and make the decision which will best serve the total set of needs of the family, not just the financial aspect.

The decisions you make as a husband may be popular and well received by your wife, or they may not be well received. How your wife will react is *not* the determining factor in what you decide. Don't decide something just to let your wife have her own way. You should take her views into account, but you should base your decision on what you think is *right*, not on how it will be received.

Don't let the fear of making a mistake keep you from making a decision. You aren't perfect, and God doesn't expect you to be (your wife does, maybe, but never God). Fear of mistakes can either paralyze you into indecision or cause you to push the decision onto your wife. Don't shirk the decision-making responsibility God has placed on you. You will make fewer and fewer mistakes as you grow in wisdom and in listening to the Lord. But you will never grow in wisdom if you don't start making decisions in spite of your fear.

A word about delegation. The husband doesn't have to make *all* the decisions. In fact, there are many he shouldn't make because they belong properly to his wife's domain. Menu planning, how the kitchen cupboards are arranged, when to feed the baby, house decor, and many other matters are her business. It's all right to give her your input on the matter, but she should make these decisions unless you have some serious reason for making them yourself.

How often you need to make decisions or give direction will vary depending on the circumstances of your marriage. But you will have to make them, since you are the head of the family.

5. *Discipline the children and train them to honor and respect their mother.*

Fathers have the main responsibility to discipline the children. Every father has the responsibility, as the head of the family, to see that wrongdoing is punished. Too many fathers leave this job to their wives. Some don't want to be bothered, some don't want to be the "heavy" with their children (although they are perfectly happy to let their wife be the "heavy"), and others think that raising the children is basically the wife's responsibility.

Scripture makes it clear (Eph 6:4; Col 3:21) that while parents raise children together, the father is ultimately responsible. Specifically, he is the one who should discipline the children. For a sobering look at how God holds fathers accountable for their children, read the story of Eli and his sons in 1 Samuel 2:12-36.

Sometimes the mother needs to administer the discipline because the father isn't home. This is especially true with young children. That is appropriate, but the father should administer most discipline himself and he should make sure that when his wife does it, it's done consistently and effectively.

The father should also make certain that he is training his children to properly honor their mother. You should see that they speak and act respectfully toward her. You need to *teach* them how to do it, since they have no natural inclination to do so. You should set a good example yourself in respectful speech. Don't correct your wife in front of the children or engage in unrighteous speech.

One man I know tried for years without success to get his children to speak respectfully to their mother. He never recognized that they were simply doing what they heard him do. Those kids never will change until he does.

6. *See that your wife's needs are being met.* We saw in Ephesians 5 that husbands are to love and care for their wives as they do their own bodies. When you have a need (sex, relaxation, exercise, sleep), you do your best to meet that need. Are you as eager to see that your wife has her needs met? Most men leave their wives to fend for themselves. The pattern of Christ's relationship with his church is very different. He tends the church, cares for it, and doesn't neglect its needs. When you got married, you took on the responsibility to see that another person's needs were met.

Of course, not every desire or preference is a need—whether for your wife or yourself. Be discerning. If your wife expresses the "need" to spend a month by herself in Florida in January while you take care of the five kids in Minnesota, she's probably expressing a desire. Her real need is for a break.

Even when your wife has a legitimate need, sometimes it cannot be immediately met. Your wife may need some time by herself, but the circumstances of your lives may not allow it to happen right away. You may have to do some planning to get it to happen in the near future.

The point I want to emphasize is that you, as the husband and head, have the responsibility to see that your wife's needs are being met. Here is a list of the more important needs for husbands to be concerned about.

—*Sex.* Because a man's sexual response is usually faster than a woman's, you may slip into a "quickie" meet-my-needs attitude toward sex and neglect to take the time to bring your wife to sexual satisfaction. Chapter eight talks about this area more completely. I mention it here to point out that satisfying your wife's sexual needs is an often-neglected area of the husband's responsibility.

—*Time with other Christian women.* Our wives need to spend some time with other Christian women for friendship and support. We should not expect them to persevere alone. They should have supportive relationships with other Christian women, and it is *your* responsibility to make sure that they do.

—*Take the "load" off periodically.* Several years ago, my friend Ted gave me some excellent advice. He has been married about as long as I have been alive. In a conversation over lunch one day he said, "You know, one of the things I do for my wife from time to time is take her away from home for a weekend. We go to a motel with a pool and a nice restaurant, and I just let her relax—no cooking, cleaning, kids, phone. I do my best to make it as enjoyable for her as I can. You ought to do that for Therese."

I followed Ted's advice, and I have never regretted it. Financially, we can afford to do this about once a year, but it's still an excellent way for me to ease the burdens on Therese.

I also regularly take Therese out for dinner. I will also periodically tell her to not bother cooking a big dinner—cold sandwiches on paper plates are fine.

All of these things can help break the pressure and monotony of the housework grind and bring refreshment to your wife.

7. *Build her self-esteem through compliment and encouragement.* An important function of a husband's headship is to see that his wife is growing in self-confidence, esteem, and her ability to fulfill her role as wife and mother. This happens as he encourages her and tells her that she is doing a good job. Unfortunately, husbands have a great difficulty giving their wives encouragement. When was the last time you paid your wife a legitimate compliment? Not a distracted "Hmm, that's nice," nor a backdoor "This stew's not bad," but a genuine, full-fledged "Dear, that was a great meal," or "Say, you really look pretty tonight," or "You did an excellent job refinishing that table." Better yet, when was the last time you told her she was a good wife or a good mother and listed the reasons you think so?

Husbands should build up their wives through encouragement, not tear them down through criticism. You will have to correct your wife at times, but that is different from criticism. Correction brings about constructive change, since it is aimed at the other person's good or the good of the overall situation. On the other hand, criticism and fault-finding come from wanting to vent our gripes about things that bother *us*. They lead to bitterness, resentment, and retaliation.

8. *Take leisure time with her every week.* Much of what we have been discussing so far in this book has revolved around the functional aspects of marriage—how to make sure that the many things which must get done actually take place. Indeed, much of marriage is functional; a lot needs to happen. But husband and wife should not relate together only when there is a specific task to be accomplished or a particular need to be met. You and your wife should grow in a relationship of love simply by spending leisure time together without necessarily talking about problems or schedules or children or whatever. We highly recommend that you take leisure time together every week. Take a couple of hours or a whole evening if possible to relax together and do something you would both enjoy: take a walk; go to a play, concert, or movie; go bowling or rollerskating; scout out the best ice cream parlors in town; take a drive in the country; play Scrabble, or gin rummy, or cribbage, or (if you're "with it") Trivial Pursuit.

The important idea here is that the *two* of you take some relaxed, leisure time just to be together and enjoy one another. Some people call this "date night"; others call it "our time together." It doesn't have to take place in the evening, although that may be the most convenient time for many of you. Find the time that works best for you. This may be one of those times you vary from week to week to take greatest advantage of those things you most enjoy doing.

Once again, it's the husband's responsibility to see that leisure time happens. I guarantee you will make your wife a happy woman when you make it a weekly happening.

Our goal in this chapter has been to explore some of the key ways husbands fulfill their service in headship. Headship is hard work, isn't it? I wonder how many of us would have signed on for marriage if we had known all this beforehand. Maybe we would have echoed the disciples' words in Matthew 19:10, "If that is the case between man and wife, it is better not to marry." (NAB)

True, headship is hard work and a great responsibility, but it is also a great joy. As we see our wives flourish through our care for them—that is a cause for joy. As our homes become more peaceful and ordered—that too is a cause for joy. As we see our children growing in discipline and respect, is that not a reason for joy? Most important of all, joy comes from knowing that we, as husbands, are fulfilling the role God has assigned to us. After all, where is greater joy to be found than in doing the will of God?

To Do This Week
(Mainly for Husbands)

Individual Time

Answer the questions:
1. Did I pray for my spouse and our marriage this week?

2. Think about how you can better serve your wife in the long haul in the following areas:

  Children's training and discipline

  Decision making

  Her personal needs

  Building her self-esteem

3. Now make a specific decision about doing one concrete thing in each of those four areas this coming week.

4. Schedule leisure time for this week. Plan to do something your wife really would like to do.

5. Ask your wife to tell you the one area in your life together where you could serve her better. Decide how you can get it to happen and start working on it.

6. List the five things you most like and appreciate in your wife. Now tell her what they are and give as much detail as possible.

For further reading:

James Dobson, *What Wives Wish Their Husbands Knew about Women* (Wheaton, Ill.: Tyndale House, 1975).

At Your Service:
How Wives Love
Their Husbands

ONE DAY, WHILE I (Therese) was planning this book, I told a group of women what Randy and I hoped to accomplish with it. They all enthusiastically agreed that it was "really needed." Then they began to shoot questions about what they hoped would be included in it. "How about communication?" "What about helping men *understand* us?" "What about when you *really* disagree?" and so on.

Afterwards something was nudging me internally. Something was missed in our discussion. What was the missing piece? Over the dinner dishes, when I was alone, it occurred to me that unless a woman has a personal, interior strength, all the information in the world isn't going to be enough to make any difference. All the advice in the world, all the wisdom on earth will be nothing more than another "how to" approach to marriage if there is not something *more* going on internally.

Before we can talk about how to love and serve our husbands, we need to pause a moment and do some personal "housecleaning."

Personal Strength to Serve

Several years ago, I did some research for an article for a Christian magazine about how wives can support their husbands' Christian commitment. I asked ten men what they thought were the most important ways that their wives support them. I have to admit that I was a bit curious to see how men experienced it from their side. While my survey was less than scientific, I did come up with one clear result. Without exception, all the husbands said that the most important way their wives could support their Christian commitment was to have a strong, daily relationship with God. That made more of a difference to them than anything else their wives did.

Besides wanting the best for their wives (and what is better than a relationship with God?), they all confessed that when things were working well spiritually for their wives, it had an effect on their husband's life as well as on the whole family.

I found this response a bit humbling. My relationship with God was not only important for my own "personal" life, but it was crucial for my husband's and children's lives as well. I made my personal time of prayer and scripture an even higher priority than before. Other lives depended on me!

Marriage is a tremendous challenge. In order to live and love the way that God is calling us to, we need to be in touch with God—the source of life and love itself. Otherwise we will be struggling and using "white-knuckle" power to get through each day.

If you don't have a daily time with the Lord—get one! It will be the most important thing you can do. I know all the things that work against having a regular time with God. With five children ranging in age from two to fourteen, my life is very full.

After the birth of our last child, night feedings and nocturnal visits from our then two-year-old kept me feeling exhausted. I kept saying to myself, "As soon as Rebecca starts sleeping through the night, *then* I'll get up early and pray before anyone is awake." Then teething wakefulness gave way to ear infections; I still didn't get a good night's sleep. I realized that I might never pray again if I waited until circumstances were "right" for prayer. Circumstances would always hinder prayer. I saw what was happening. I was using the word "circumstances" for the word "excuses." Prayer couldn't be seen as an option—it was a necessity.

This is true for every stage in your life.

A Wife's Role—To Follow Where He Leads

While the husband certainly carries the responsibilities of being the head of the family, the wife can make marriage a joyful journey together to the Lord or a joyless trial. For marriage to work right you should not only love your husband in thought and word and deed, but submit to his family leadership in thought, in word, and in deed.

Randy and I joke about how I always submit to his decisions—the punch line of the joke is "unless I disagree." Years ago, this was no joke. There was one point in our life when Randy thought one thing ought to happen and I thought *exactly* the opposite. Usually, after time and lots of communication, we are able to resolve such disagreements. This time, though, we were running out of time. As the deadline came closer and closer we seemed to grow further and further apart in our approaches to this problem.

I knew that I needed to submit to Randy's discernment. But on an emotional level, I just knew that all types of horrible things would happen if we didn't do it *my* way—it seemed so right.

When the time for the decision came, Randy began to move in the direction he felt the Lord wanted us to, and I became more melancholy. I knew that I couldn't go on feeling this way. Our life, our relationships, my relationship with the Lord just wouldn't work right if I continued to feel this way. It had a deadening effect on our whole life. I rather hoped that my dire predictions would come true to prove that my way was better.

I prayed knowing that I had a bad attitude. The Lord, in his mercy to me, cut through all my hurt pride, defenses, and anger, and said, "If you want to keep acting this way, you will have a miserable future and most likely your dreary predictions will come to pass. Or you can submit to Randy's leadership in your family and relate to it as if he was following my will. Then support that decision actively with your thoughts, with your actions, and with your speech."

How could I do that? Well, I just decided to *do* it hoping that it wasn't too phony sounding. (Remember, I still believed I was right.) As I professed with my mouth and *actively* supported my husband's decision with thought and deed, amazing things happened.

First the spiritual and emotional tone of the house changed drastically—for the better—overnight. I experienced the grace to follow Randy in the right spirit. God's way for peace in the family worked. My husband needed to lead the family, and it was my duty and responsibility to follow—in thought, in word, and in deed.

Later Randy said that he knew that he had to do what was right even if I had continued to act like a brat (my words). But our life was far better when I decided to trust God and to trust him.

Most of the time Randy and I work out the direction of our lives together in a normal way—through conversations, common experiences, the daily living of life that husbands and wives do. Decisions usually get made in a very "normal" way too. But every once in a while, whether it is a major turn in our life or in a small, less dramatic way, we don't agree. Then I pray that once again God will give me a humble and courageous spirit to support my husband, not only externally, but in thought, in word, and in deed. And he has never failed to provide the grace I need to die to my "great" ideas or my wounded pride or "righteous" anger.

And the fruit? A mutual love and respect that grows deeper every day.

Is this asking the impossible? No. Trust in God and trust in your husband is the number one priority for any woman.

But *trust* is an important word in any Christian woman's vocabulary.

Trusting God

It is critical for a woman to know without doubt that she can trust God with *her* life, with her husband's life, with their family life.

Trust seems to be one of those essentials that must be working right before a woman can get on with other things. A woman needs to decide that *God does love her,* personally, and that she can trust him with every thing and every person in her life. He is *trustworthy*. He is big enough for any problem. He has the power and the wisdom to care for her and her concerns.

The best comes forth in a woman who trusts God. Why? Because a woman's life as a wife and a mother is one that places such a demand on her resources that she is acutely aware that her love and energy are *not* enough to see her through. When she lays down her burden, her fears, her anxieties and looks to God—the giver of all, the father of all—she gains strength from her trust in *Him*

A woman's trust in God is her strength. Without it she is vulnerable to fear and anxiety. With it she is truly the giver of life to all she loves.

Trust Your Husband!

Because of God's wonderful plan for our marriages, we need to have a similar disposition toward our husbands. We need to trust them in order to live the kind of unity God is calling us to.

However, many women may have more difficulty trusting their husbands than trusting God. In fact a friend of mine once said, "*God,* I can trust! He's perfect. But my husband . . . That's another story! I *know* he makes mistakes."

Here are some reasons that I've heard women give for not trusting their husbands. See if you can hear yourself in any of these examples. I know I do.

1. He is not spiritual enough. (I've been a Christian longer than he has.)

2. He still has faults. (I'll trust him when he's perfect.)

3. He has made mistakes with our life in the past. (How can I ever trust him again?)

4. I've been hurt so many times in my past I can't open myself to it again. (My father and then my husband disappointed me, and I can never trust men again.)

5. I'm better at decision-making than he is anyway. (How can I trust him when I know I'm right and he's wrong?)

Now, here are some good reasons to trust your husband and some suggestions to help you do so.

We will always find good reasons not to do something that is either hard to do or that we don't *want* to do. We need to be honest with ourselves. If we decide to live our lives according to God's plan, then he will give us the grace and the help we need to do it. We are not just left to our own selves and whatever meager resources we can muster. We are children of God, and he not only shows us the way but also gives us everything we need to walk that way. What are you trusting in when you trust your husband? *You* are trusting in God. You are trusting that when you live your life with God's plan for peace, he will provide and protect you and your life. You are trusting your husband because that is what God is asking you to do.

Ask yourself this question. Are some of your reasons for not trusting God or your husband really excuses? We can easily avoid doing the right things by making excuses that sound very reasonable. Be honest and have faith that God is in charge. Personally, that thought gives me much more security than if I thought that *I* was in charge.

Most women have a very strong drive to be in control of their lives and the lives of others. I've found that some women need to correct this sometimes overactive drive by letting go. *Let go* of being right; *let go* of being more spiritual; *let go* of being hurt; *let go* of analyzing your husband's faults. *Let go* of being in control, and *let God* have his way in your life and in your marriage.

This decision does not make your husband perfect or more spiritual or more sensitive. This decision does not erase years of mistakes and hurt. It *does* put you and your husband in the right relationship to God and to each other. It gives the Holy Spirit room to work and move in both of you.

Only one person can be in charge—let it be God!

Dianne told me her story: "A major area of tension in our marriage has been our budget. For many years I took care of the bills and household funds. There was always a problem with the way money flowed when Jerry was in charge. Each time he was in charge, the budget fell apart and I would take it back to 'save' us from sure bankruptcy.

"It drove me crazy to see how things fell apart when he took over. I'd get angry and resentful as I saw our carefully built savings vanish.

"One day Jerry said that the Lord wanted him to take over the finances. My first thought was 'Oh, no, not again.' But this time he insisted, saying that the Lord showed him that he had to get this area into order.

"For six months I said nothing, expecting the bill collectors at any moment. But it worked. God did speak to my husband and put an area of our family life in order that had been a constant source of frustration. It was God's timing, not mine.

"Be free to trust. Trust that God is in charge and has a better plan for our lives than the one I had. When it was God's timing—it worked. I actually distracted God's work with my own nagging and pushing for a change that I thought was important, rather than waiting on God."

Energy to Serve

God created his women to be a blessing and to give life through their love.

In fact Paul in his letter to Timothy presents the ideal quite well. "Women should adorn themselves modestly and sensibly in seemly apparel, not with braided hair or gold or pearls or costly attire, but by good deeds as befits women who profess religion" (1 Tm 2:9, 10). And in the first letter of Peter, chapter 3: "Let not yours be the outward adorning with braiding of hair, decoration of gold, and wearing of fine clothing, but let it be the hidden person of the heart with the imperishable jewel of a gentle and quiet spirit."

Our lives should be filled with the eagerness to do good deeds trusting and loving God. It is the inner heart, the inner spirit, that radiates beauty, not the latest hair style nor the newest in clothes. It is the heart of the Christian wife that shows the beauty of God and pleases her husband.

Yet it is important to be good stewards of our bodies. Some women let themselves go. Good nutrition and staying within the right weight range for our height and age is one of those basics that should be operating in a woman's life. The motivation for this is both to please God in our good stewardship of the body he gave us and a right desire to be pleasing to our husbands. Another factor is that we need simple, human, physical energy to live out commitments cheerfully and with a good attitude.

It takes all the resources I can muster each day to love everyone (or even *most* people) in my life. If I'm not eating right, sleeping right, and feeling good about myself, then it's much more difficult to stay patient with my children, be loving toward my husband, and to be charitable in listening to a particularly talkative woman I know.

God created his women to give *life* to those they come into contact with. That "life" she gives, God's life, shouldn't depend on the fluctuations of her eating habits, weight, or physical energy. Women are too important to God's plan for marriage to be tired and run down. We get into shape and eat right in order to serve God, not to satisfy a worldly beauty standard.

Emotions

When we were talking about this chapter, my husband was quick to say that the more a wife's emotions are in order, the more peacefully the whole family works. Many women have said to me that when their emotions are working right, so many other areas that are potential difficulties seem to run much more smoothly. A book I wrote several years ago, *The Facts about Your Feelings,* covers this area in much greater depth. I suggest it for every woman who wants to serve her husband and family.

Joy—A Grateful Heart

A cheerful attitude is another of those strengths that women should seek to develop. Women say to me that they just don't have the right kind of personality to be cheerful. My response to that is that cheerfulness is an *attitude,* not a personality trait.

How can a woman develop a cheerful attitude? Cheerfulness and joyfulness come from a *grateful heart.* It is out of the heart that the mouth speaks and the woman appears. A woman who wakes every day knowing that she is loved by God and that she is in his hands just naturally develops a cheerful attitude. Everything that she has and needs is generously provided by him. She is thankful. Thankful for her life, for the people in it, and the gift of Jesus that makes all this possible. With a heart full of love and thankfulness, a woman cannot help but bring life and joy to every situation.

Part II—Love in Action

"The life has gone out of our marriage. Something's wrong. I don't know what it is or what to do about it!"

The woman who spoke these words to me was in a marriage that was not "bad" but was very far from satisfying. As the very real responsibilities of marriage and family accumulated in their lives, this couple's relationship had evolved into a very functional "ma and pa" arrangement: "He does this and I do that."

I've found that it's not uncommon for both men and women to be at a loss about how to express love to one another after the courtship and "honeymoon" stage is over. Most of us can run off a list rather quickly of romantic expressions—flowers, candy, loving words, passionate embraces. But other than these traditionally "romantic" expressions, we can rapidly come to a halt when it comes to practical expressions of love in marriage. A void can form after the high intensity of the romantic period ends.

Here are some principles that can help women know how to express their love in marriage: 1) put your love into action; and 2) custom design it to fit your husband. Love is often viewed as an emotion that is expressed either sexually or verbally. Women are often comfortable with verbal expression as the major avenue of expressing love. While I'm all for verbal and sexual expression in marriage, I believe that one daily expression is often lacking—love through actions.

Love in action is not a lesson that we need to commit to memory but a way of life centered on the question "How can I show my love to *this* man today?"

What does it mean to custom design your love in action to your husband? First think about the specific man that you are married to. Give thought to who *he* is and how *he* would experience being loved. Women sometimes develop a picture of a generic-brand husband that we fit our theories of love to rather than the real man we are married to. The way that I would custom design my love to Randy *should* be different from the way that you would express your love to your husband.

Ask yourself these questions.

1. *Do I put my love on my knees?* The most important service that I can provide any person that I love is to pray and intercede for him. What better way can I put love for husband into action than to pray for him. I've found it helpful to ask Randy if there are any specific things I can bring to the Lord for him. It might be a difficult job situation, finances, relationship problems, clarity on a tough problem he's working on, anything that can be on his mind that I can support in prayer.

2. *Do I respect my husband?* "And let each wife see that she respects her husband" (Eph 5:33). After ten full verses of instruction to the husbands about how to love, care for, and cherish their wives, Paul simply states "and let each wife see that she respects her husband." Obviously that is a pretty important statement about a major duty of a wife.

One of the greatest services that a woman can do for her husband is to respect him—in thought, in word, and in action. All three are necessary because they are interrelated. What you think affects what you speak, and what you speak affects how you act. No matter what shortcomings your husband may have, no matter how many changes he needs to make—always speak and think and act in a respectful way. The way you speak of him and act around him influences the way your children will perceive their father. It also influences the way other men and women think and behave toward your husband. It will also deeply influence the disposition of your heart.

I've also found that the encouragement and support a woman gives her husband is part of the gift of *life* that women can give to their husbands. Your husband needs someone who believes in him. He does not need someone who believes that he's perfect, but someone who knows him intimately—his good points and his failings—and *still believes in him.*

Put respect in action. Don't just agree that you should show respect, but actually begin to *act and speak and think* with respect. Be sincere. Don't tell your husband that he has great talent in an area where he is obviously weak. Point out his real strong points and let him know how much you do appreciate them.

3. *Do you cook for your husband, or do you cook for yourself or according to food fads that are in vogue?* This might sound *too* practical, but I've found that men experience love from their wives when they prepare food they like. All good homemakers should make casseroles and cook vegetables, right? Well, my husband dislikes casseroles and thinks that the worst thing that can happen to a vegetable is to cook it. For years I tried to think up new ways to make casseroles and ways to slip some cooked vegetables into his mouth. Finally, he said in desperation, "Will you just please stop trying to trick me into eating things that I don't like."

I also thought that men should like a large variety of main courses, so I would try to dazzle Randy with a wide variety of dinners. One day, while we were talking about food, he hesitantly asked if we couldn't have spaghetti and meatballs more often and not have so many new things. I managed to resist the temptation to be justly hurt over his lack of appreciation for "all that I had done for him," and saw that I needed to cook for *him,* not according to my picture of how things *ought* to work. So I've stopped trying to trick Randy into eating tofu meatballs and left him smiling contentedly over the meat sauce.

4. *Do you do the things he's asked you to do?* Do you do them joyfully? Women often complain about the irritation they experience when their husbands "intrude" in their daily routines and ask them to do a few things for them. Sometimes my first reaction is to feel put out. I had already had

my day mentally arranged and mildly resented the intrusion of his request. No, it's not a *big* resentment, nor are they *big* requests either. Just normal errands: to make a bank deposit, to stop at the post office, or to pick up a tire at the garage.

Yet our love and commitment are shown to our families in the small expressions of joyful service. Instead of being swift to be "put out," we need to see those practical requests as specific ways we can show our love to *this* man *this* day.

In his letter to Timothy, Paul describes the qualities that a widow should exhibit. Traditionally the church sees these qualities as a general model for all women to emulate.

"She must be well attested for her good deeds, as one who has brought up children, shown hospitality, washed the feet of the saints, relieved the afflicted, and devoted herself to doing good in every way" (1 Tm 5:10).

The Lord had shown me that I needed to apply these qualities to my husband and my children. All scripture needs to be applied to our lives twenty-four hours a day. Again the *agape*-love is love in action.

5. *Does your time for relaxation together express his interest and hobbies?* Shortly after the birth of our third child in five years it occurred to me that it had been a long time since my husband had done any fishing. Circumstances had whittled our personal time together to a bare minimum. We usually spent it at home semicomatose on the couch, talking or reading. One Friday afternoon, I arranged for a babysitter, and instead of volunteering to pick the restaurant to go out to, I ordered a pizza, threw his old clothes and fishing tackle for two into the back of the car, and picked Randy up from work. We ate pizza and drank pop by the river and fished. Randy was stunned at first by our evening out. I enjoyed it too. I came away from the evening relaxed from the change of pace and rather exhilarated from catching my first twelve-inch bass! You may need to use a little creativity, but the joy of making your husband happy is reward enough.

6. *Do you approach your sexual life thinking of how you can serve him?* More about this in a later chapter. Briefly, we need to apply the same principle of love in action here as well. How can I custom-design my love-making to love and please this man?

7. *When he's sick, do you cheerfully serve him?* One friend of mine said that the most difficult time she had in loving her husband was when he was sick

and in bed. Not all women experience this, but I know that a number of women do. Usually the response is one of impatience. Women can think, "I have enough to do with sick children, the groceries, and the laundry. It's a hassle to have to take you into account too." Instead, look at this time as a special time when you have a unique opportunity to love and serve him—again *love in action*. Thank God that you have this special way to express your love to your husband. This kind of loving service reminds me of the Lord washing the feet of the disciples at the last supper. What a wonderful opportunity to love in the midst of our busy lives!

8. *Do you impose feminine standards on your husband?* As a service to both yourself and to your husband, let him be a man. It is with wry humor that I think of all the women I know, myself included, who were attracted to a man, married him, and then methodically tried to change him to fit rather neatly into a feminine world. I was brought up in an east coast family where the four girls in the family emerged into adulthood equipped with very strong feelings about what was "proper" behavior and what wasn't. Typically masculine behavior and interests were not a part of my neatly defined world. My world was "right," so his world and ways must therefore be "wrong."

I learned that I had to stop trying to change his masculine ways to fit my very feminine definition of life. One example stands out vividly—weekend sports on television. On weekends, Randy assumed that if a "good game" was on TV, he would watch it. My initial reaction was one of horror: "What a waste of a perfectly good afternoon!" I tried to change him to the "right" way—mine. We could be doing so many more useful and worthwhile things like more chores around the house and shopping.

After I realized that watching weekend TV sports was a perfectly normal male interest, I had to decide how to respond. Some women give up in disgust, and the issue becomes part of the indirect tug-of-war that can go on within marriages. Instead I chose to sometimes do things that I'd like to do by myself or with a friend, and sometimes I curl up next to Randy on the couch and watch the games with him. I have found it quality snuggling time and a wonderful time to informally chat—during commercials, of course. Over the years I've even developed a few favorite teams that *I* make it a point to watch.

I've found that other hobbies or interests can be seen the same way. Sports, fishing, hunting, and movies are some of the male favorites that women can have difficulties with. Differences can threaten our picture of "oneness." Unity doesn't mean being the *same*—same interests, same preferences.

9. *Do you know his preferences?* Several years ago the Lord showed me that the true way of love is a generous one. Real love does not keep a scorecard and doesn't insist on a contract of mutual obligations. I realized I should actively seek his preferences and do them, not as part of a *law* that I have to follow but as a beautiful expression of my love for him. Again love in action!

A good example is the way I cut my hair and the use of make-up. My husband does not have a lot of strong preferences about relatively superficial things. But he does have a few preferences about the length of my hair. I would like the shortest cut possible for summer. But Randy prefers it longer. He would not make a big fuss if I cut my hair shorter than he likes, but he would prefer it longer. I decided to follow his preference.

Randy also prefers that I use as little make-up as possible; he says that he likes me just the way I am. I follow this preference too, even when I'm in the mood for a "different look." After all, I can take delight in the fact that my husband likes me just being me.

10. *Do you resent his time away from you?* You and your husband need to spend time together, away from the phone and children, but men also need time with other Christian men, just as women need time with other Christian women. Some men, though, watch sports *excessively* at the expense of their family relationships.

A husband and wife can put pressure on one another to be *everything* to each other, and that is impossible. We need a husband—not a man playing the role of a good girlfriend. He needs a wife—and male companions as well. Sometimes, just knowing that can take the pressure off the marriage.

Sometimes a woman may think her husband's friends and time spent in sports are *competing* with her. Instead, we need to see this time as one of the many factors that enrich our lives and bring something more to the marriage. When I come home from playing tennis, I feel invigorated and not so wrapped up in the problems with the washing machine. And when my husband comes home from being with other Christian men, he enjoys my feminine company and appreciates it for what it is.

11. *Is home a place of peace and refreshment?* Women can make coming home a joy or another challenge at the end of the day. Use your creativity

and your love to guide you. Put your love in action here. Is your husband greeted by a woman who welcomes him with love and joy, or is he met with a haggard, complaining woman? Now I don't mean a phony smile and an artificial welcome. I mean a genuine "Gosh, I'm glad you're home." Don't follow the greeting with a list of the horrible things that happened during the day that he needs to deal with. Give him a welcome, then give him some space. Give him a few moments to wash up or take off his coat and change his clothes. Train your children to stop what they're doing and get up and greet their father appropriately. You may need to bite your tongue about the plugged toilet or the broken window, but let his coming home be the high point of his day.

Home should be a place that is physically pleasing to our husbands. Sometimes women decorate their homes to express their tastes or personality and don't think about the comfort of their husbands. When we shop for furniture, Randy tests it for comfort while I look at style. It takes us longer to make a purchase, but our home is a place for men and women.

I've also found that men like one place in the house where they can put their feet up at the end of the day, read their Bible, watch a ball game, or read a book to a child.

Home should also be a place where both men and women can bring their friends and know that they will be greeted with love and respect. One good friend told me that one of the nicest things that her husband had said to her was that he was proud to bring his friends home because it never seemed to be an imposition and they were always made to feel welcome. And my friend has six children! One of the other men had said that his wife would "kill him" if he ever brought friends home. It is the *attitude* that makes a difference.

Love gives life. Some people might say you are crazy to live your life this way. Isn't it foolish to give yourself to someone this way—to serve your husband! Surely you're going to be taken advantage of! What about *you?* Who's going to think of you?

Outside the context of a Christian marriage this way of love is a big risk. But in Christ it makes all the sense in the world. It's a spiritual principle to love unconditionally; love begets love, life begets life. As you serve your husband in a womanly way, he will love you as a husband does. And God is blessing you for your loving heart. What a great way to get yourself taken care of!

Remember the story of the unhappy woman I opened the chapter with? I gave her a version of this chapter, and she followed it over a period of a few months. She still can't believe what love in action can do to a marriage. The life that was missing in their marriage is being rekindled. She is learning to love her husband as a wife should, and he is learning to love and care for her as a husband should.

Putting your love in action is a whole lifestyle, not just a one-time pepper-upper to a marriage.

A wife's call in marriage can be summed in this way. A wife is called to:

Be a Blessing not a Curse

Bring Healing not Hurt

Encourage not to Discourage

Give Life not Death to All She Meets

Reflect God's Life in All She Does

To Do This Week (Mainly for Wives)

Individual Time

Answer the questions:

1. Did I pray for my spouse and our marriage this week?

2. In the first section of "Strength to Serve" spend time looking at each of the areas mentioned

—Relationship with God

—Relationship with husband; trust, letting go

—Physically

—Emotionally

—Cheerful attitude

3. Decide to improve one or two things in each area. Be decisive!

4. Love in Action
How can I "custom design" my love for *this man,* my husband?

1. Prayer	7. When he's sick
2. Respect	8. Feminine standards?
3. Cook	9. Preferences
4. Serve him practically	10. Time away
5. Relaxation	11. Home, a place of peace
6. Sexual life	

5. Tell your husband three things you especially like about him or respect him for.

For further reading:

Joyce Landorf, *Any Woman Can Be More Beautiful* (New York: Piller Books, 1975).

Therese Cirner, *The Facts about Your Feelings* (Ann Arbor: Servant Books, 1982).

Gladys Hunt, *Ms. Means Myself* (Grand Rapids: Zondervan, 1975).

Karen Mains, *Open Heart, Open Home* (Elgin, Ill.: David C. Cook, 1976).

Week Eight

Affection and Sex

ITS ALMOST AMUSING how the subject of sex arouses people's curiosity. Editors know this. Almost everyone reads articles in magazines and newspapers about the latest findings on sexual behavior or about the latest technique to revitalize your sex life.

Women's magazines and the national scandal papers scream the latest amazing finding about new erogenous zones with the same enthusiasm as the latest cure for cancer. Many people measure their self-worth by whether their sexual lives measure up to the latest statistics on sexual performance.

Sex has been taken out of the bedroom and put into the headlines and into the laboratories. Sexuality is marked by a tremendous self-consciousness. Do we have enough orgasms? If you have one, is it good enough? Is it often enough? Is it the right kind?

Our sex lives have been charted, measured, and reported; graphed, photographed, and analyzed. This "scientific approach" to sex has some distinct drawbacks:

1. It makes us tremendously self-conscious about our sexual performance.

2. It creates a significant anxiety about being "normal"—whatever that is.

3. We get frustrated because our sexual experience doesn't have the billboard glamour night after night and year after year that it is "supposed" to have.

4. We can start blaming ourself or our spouse for being the "cause" of the problem.

A satisfying sex life is seen as the measure of success in a relationship. The lack of it is often presented as justifiable grounds for adultery or divorce.

Let's change the questions and the forum for discussion. Let's put sex back into the bedroom and make it a wonderfully private affair between the three of you.

Three of us? Yes, the two of you and God.

As always, God does have a better plan than one we think of ourselves—a plan that has less anxiety attached to it. It's a plan that fits into the rest of our lives in harmony.

Our culture presents sex as the definition of a happy and successful marriage. God's purpose and plan for marriage—communication, service to one another, *agape* love—are the *real* measures of a truly successful marriage. Sex is a blessing from God to a man and a woman in marriage. But it is not the standard by which you measure the success of your marriage or your personal worth.

Can you imagine the questions the Father will ask us on judgment day. Will he ask, "How often did you have intercourse last week? How intense was your orgasm?" Of course not. He will ask how loving and charitable we were to each other and if we lived every day for him.

What *is* God's plan?

Affectionate affection.—Be affectionate! Affection for one another is part of the blessing and joy that God gives marriages. There certainly is *agape* love, an emphasis on service and commitment, and of course there is sexual attraction. But these are not the only ways to express our love and care and attraction for one another. There is plain old-fashioned affection.

Verbal and *physical* affection are two ways to build up your personal relationship. Words of appreciation, of love, as well as affectionate hugs and kisses (that aren't designed with an ulterior motive) are splendid ways to express that you're really glad you're married and that you just appreciate your spouse.

Differences between men's and women's personal preferences show up in the way we express affection. Everyone needs to hear positive words about how they are doing and just how much they are loved. Women usually like to hear the specific words like "I love *you*" and "You're still the prettiest woman at the party tonight!" Men need to hear "I love you" too, but not usually as deeply or as often as women.

Physical affection provides richness for a marriage. Holding hands, an affectionate back rub, snuggling on the couch watching your favorite show (instead of in "his" and "hers" chairs), the affectionate kisses in greeting one another all contribute their small but important share of life to a marriage.

It's also healthy for children to see their parents display appropriate verbal and physical affection in front of them.

Women especially seem to thrive in their sexual relationship with their husband when there is a healthy dose of nonforeplay affection—that is, verbal and physical affection from their husbands without the obvious goal of bed as the next stop. Some women stop expressing any affection for their husbands because the husbands always take it as a sexual proposition. Don't let that happen to you!

When affirmation and affection are woven into the whole fabric of the relationship, the relationship as a whole has more life, and the sexual relationship is more satisfying too.

Scripture and Christian tradition teach that there are three purposes for sex in a Christian marriage.

1. The sexual relationship is biologically designed for bearing children. The basic function of intercourse is to bring the sperm and the egg together in order to create new life; a new member of the family of God and of your family. This is an unpopular side of sex today. Our culture often sees pregnancy as an ever-present "threat," the bane of the human race. Thus we have abortion as the final act of preventing a new little life from joining the family of God.

In his book *Sexual Suicide* the sociologist George Gilder refers to the divorce between sex and procreation this way. "While sex is given a steadily larger role (by society in general) it loses contact with its procreative sources and becomes increasingly promiscuous and undifferentiated....It becomes in essence a form of sensual massage." We thought it interesting that a sociologist could identify in a non-Christian presentation the very heart of the Christian context of sex in marriage.

2. Release of sexual tension and the proper context for sexual pleasure is one of the blessings in marriage. God placed a sexual drive in men and women and designed marriage as the appropriate place to express it.

3. Sexual intercourse is a beautiful way to express love and affection and appreciation for one another. It is a form of love that surpasses the limitations of words, a form that expresses the mutual love, affection, and unity that a husband and a wife share in the midst of all the responsibilities and hard work of their daily lives.

A Uniquely Christian Sexual Problem

Some Christians look at enjoying sex as wrong. They have a sort of "if-it-feels-good-then-it-must-be-from-the-devil" point of view. This attitude can come from misplaced emphases in some Christian groups, strict parental upbringing, or from a misunderstanding of scripture.

God intended the sexual relationship in marriage to be a blessing and a source of joy to both the man and the woman.

One common source of confusion about sex is the way scripture uses the word "flesh." When Paul warns of the desire of the flesh, he is referring to unruly passions or desires (not only sexual ones) that are out of God's order. "Flesh" can refer to any non-Spirit-led desires—a "fleshly" desire for recognition, for wealth, for sinful sexual relationships, or for advancing one's own position.

Paul uses a different word entirely when he refers to the sexual desire of a husband and wife for each other.

Some Christians have trouble enjoying God's blessing in marital sex because of past worldly experience of sex.

Maureen had one of those dramatic testimonies. As a young woman she had led a wild and rebellious life against her parents and all of their values. She had lived with a man and lived a sordid life with him. Some deviant sexual experimentation was part of their relationship.

Several years after they had been separated, Maureen had a radical conversion experience to the Lord. She eventually had a previous marriage annulled and married a fine and devout man.

They were a very attractive couple, seemingly without a care in the world. Maureen, however, eventually shared with Therese her difficulty with coldness and lack of sexual responsiveness to her husband. She experienced little or no joy in their sex life and felt tremendously guilty that she was disappointing her loving husband. She also experienced a pretty violent reaction when her husband encouraged her to wear more attractive nightgowns to bed.

With the guidance of the Holy Spirit, it became clear that Maureen so hated her sinful past that she didn't want any of it to taint her good and holy marriage. That included sex. In an effort not to let worldly or lustful desire enter her present marriage, she was inhibiting the flow of God's good and natural blessings in their marriage.

Through talking and prayer and the healing power of the Holy Spirit, Maureen realized that she is a new creation and that the "old man" had died in baptism. She realized that she should view herself as "virginal" in heart and let her good Christian husband lead her into making love for the "first time." Thankfully, with the love and patience of her husband, she was able to experience a normal, healthy married love.

Within the setting of Christian commitment, a husband and wife can freely enjoy each other in innocence as they explore the sexual domain together.

Putting on Jesus Christ

There is a popular Christian song that says, "Put on Jesus Christ, once we were darkness now we are light. Live in daylight not in the night. Put on Jesus Christ!" Don't let your sexual relationship stay in the secular "darkness," but let it flourish in the light of Christ. This does not mean a superspiritual approach to your sex life. It means that your sex life, like all other areas of your life, should be inside the light and the life of Jesus Christ.

We have talked with quite a few couples who were surprised that God is interested in their sex lives. He *is* interested. While a healthy sex life is not the measure of a healthy marriage, it is an area that God intends as a blessing for marriages, a gift and a joy to the husband and wife.

We suggest that all couples follow the steps in this next section, whether you are newly married or celebrating your fiftieth wedding anniversary.

1. Together pray that God reveal to you *his* purpose and plan for sex in marriage. You may be surprised that you don't really have the mind of Christ for this area. Allow his Holy Spirit to reveal and teach you God's plan and purpose for marriage.

2. *Repent.* We have found that a good "house cleaning" can give that newness that most marriages need.

We suggest that both the husband and wife privately repent for past sexual sins but to not confess it to each other unless they feel a specific prompting of God to do so. Why? We have found that telling "all" rarely helps a marriage to grow into newness. However, we do highly recommend that sins against one another do get confessed to the partner and forgiveness given.

Here are some memory joggers for past sins.

sexual sins when you were young, teenagers

premarital heavy kissing and petting

premarital intercourse

masturbation

pornography

perversions; homosexuality, etc.

abortive means of birth control

abortion

extramarital sexual relationships

unfaithfulness in our hearts, if not in action

sexual fantasy

Within marriages another whole set of sinful behavior can be generally lumped together under the title "selfishness." Selfishness expresses itself sexually in a marriage by forcing or coercing your partner to have intercourse more frequently, *less frequently,* or in a way that is distasteful to your partner. It is also expressed in sexual relations that prove satisfying to only one of the partners.

Manipulation is another sin that can be found to operate in the sexual relationship. We can send out verbal or nonverbal messages that control or insure that one partner's desires or wishes get satisfied. Repentance and forgiveness is essential. Once forgiveness has been given, new life cannot come from the old unless the sin and the hurt are left in the past and not carried into the present or the future.

3. Ask the Holy Spirit to heal any internal hurts accumulated in the past that can interfere with the true childlike joy and freedom that God intends for all of his children.

Guilt from past sins and past hurtful sexual experiences, such as sexual abuse as a child, rape, or homosexual experience, can carry significant scars into a marriage without God. Healing may never occur or come only after years of counseling. But the Holy Spirit can heal in ways that are impossible for man without the power of God.

Mutual Care

First Corinthians 7:3-5: "The husband should give to his wife her conjugal rights, and likewise the wife to her husband. For the wife does not rule over her own body but the husband does; likewise the husband does not rule over his own body but the wife does. Do not refuse one another except perhaps by agreement for a season, that you may devote yourselves to prayer."

This one passage says so many things in three short verses. It states that when two people marry, their bodies no longer belong to themselves but to the other person. How radically different this is from the ideas we are exposed to every day.

The current thinking focuses on rights. You have a right to sexual fulfillment and happiness, and your purpose and happiness depend on *you* getting *your* needs met.

The Christian perspective is the opposite. Sexual fulfillment is the responsibility of your spouse. Your responsibility is to make sure that your partner's sexual needs are being met.

This works. In fact it is the perfect way for sex to work in a marriage. If you are concerned that your *spouse's* sexual needs are being met, and your spouse is concerned that *your* sexual needs are met, then everyone is taken care of. Learn what pleases your partner. Then do it. Don't do it in a self-centered me-first way, but in God's way of loving service to one another.

Once again, *agape* love is operating in every area of Christian life. No part of Christian marriage operates outside of the "other-centered" focus that mirrors God's love and care for us.

Fun or Functional?

Does that mean that sex for Christians is functional and not much fun? Not at all. The spiritual principles that operate in other areas of our life are active again in the sexual realm. As we live our lives in God's way and in his order, our lives take on a richness and a peace and a unity that are impossible to achieve through our own designs.

George Gilder comments on the current focus on pleasure. "In a quest for a better orgasm or a more intense titillation, a frustrated population goes on an ever wilder goose chase in little known erogenous zones. . . . The fact is that there is no sexual gratification more durably intense than loving genital intercourse."

Differences Again

Anyone that has been married longer than a week knows that men and women differ in sexuality just as they do in other areas of life. Men and women are different, and each particular man and woman differs from all others.

The key to unity and happiness in the sexual relationship is to 1) be glad that God made us that way; 2) discover how God intended your differences to work toward your corporate good; 3) have faith and patience as the two of you work toward the goal of sexual unity and fulfillment.

Discouragement and impatience are probably the two most destructive forces working against a couple.

Marta and Greg were married for just four years when they came to us to discuss trouble in several areas of their marriage. Finally Greg, obviously uncomfortable, confessed that Marta was very frustrated with their sexual life.

It was a pretty typical set of circumstances. Greg was easily stimulated, and it took Marta much longer to be sexually satisfied. Marta was increasingly frustrated with their love-making because she was "so slow."

She wanted to respond as quickly as Greg. She put pressure on herself to "hurry up."

Eventually tension and impatience took most of the joy out of their love-making, and Marta grew increasingly frustrated, first with herself and then with Greg in trying to solve this "problem."

Our "solution" was one that Marta wasn't expecting. We explained to her that men are more easily stimulated than women and that it was very common for the wife to need a substantial amount of foreplay. It was perfectly normal and not a "problem" to overcome. Marta was using a masculine standard for sexual response to evaluate her own sexual performance. It boiled down to "the faster, the better."

Our advice was to not only "accept" the fact that there was a difference between her and Greg, but to be expectant about how God intended that difference to work toward a full and satisfying relationship. We advised them to slow down and enjoy the early stages of love-making and not to be too "goal-oriented" and functional about it.

We are happy to report good news. Marta and Greg are living happily ever after and have found the way that these differences can work *for* them rather than against them.

A Few Suggestions

For Both of You.

1. Have a lock on your bedroom door. You do not want to be distracted by the possibility of one of the children coming in.

2. Control fantasy or busyness of your mind so that you are both emotionally and physically present to each other.

3. Be flexible and creative. A different room, different time, a different pattern of love-making will usually enhance your time together. Avoid rigid prerequisites in love-making.

4. Agree not to use time in bed to talk about family business items. Leave that for some other communication time.

For Husbands.

1. Women's sex drive is affected by many physical factors: menstruation, hormonal shifts, pregnancy, lactation and recuperation after childbirth,

and the hormonal changes that accompany menopause, as well as fatigue. Fear of pregnancy has a big effect.

2. Be more physically affectionate outside of the bedroom. Hugs, kisses, and other physical affection do more to get a woman "in the mood" when she receives them—without the goal of sexual relations—at other times of the day as well.

3. Express affection in ways other than sex—words of love and appreciation, small gifts, flowers, candlelight.

4. More leisurely foreplay. Don't get right down "to business." Spend time in preintercourse affection.

For Wives.

1. Be alert to the fact that your husband might want intercourse more frequently than you experience a need for it.

2. Husbands enjoy it when their wives sometimes initiate making love.

3. Men are visually stimulated more than women. Keep your figure in shape, your hair clean, and a sexy nightgown or underwear within reach, not just on your anniversary.

Communication Again

Sometimes it's difficult for either the husband or wife or both to actually talk about sex with each other.

Matt and Margie were married only a short time when one day, Margie observed to Therese that she certainly thought that men were very different than women. She couldn't understand why Matt wanted to make love so often. She would be happy with less frequency. After a flood of tears subsided, it was clear that they had never talked about their sex lives. It was always indirect communication. "I think he wants to." "I think she doesn't, or does she?"

We gave them suggestions on how to begin to talk about sex. It was amazing what a difference communication made for them. It can make a big difference for you too.

It's difficult to say out loud, "I like it when you do this" or "it really is irritating when you do that." Nevertheless, this kind of communication is necessary to be able to work together toward sexual happiness.

Here are a list of things that you should talk about at least once, and then periodically review:

   —How do you think things are going in our sexual relations?
   —Are you sexually satisfied?
   —What stimulates you the most—name at least two things.
   —What stimulates you the least?
   —What did we once do that you'd like to do again?
   —Is the frequency of intercourse satisfactory to both?

Serious Sexual Problems

Some Christian couples have serious sexual problems that there are no easy answers for. Some need counseling. For others we recommend patience and trust in God. Others see their sexual problems change as they grow in Christlike love and affection for one another, using the steps outlined in this book. For many Christian marriages, the sexual relationship improves with age, like good wine.

There are also a number of good Christian sexual technique books that some couples have found very helpful. We have purposely stayed away from the "how to have a better orgasm" approach because this book is not designed for that purpose, and other books cover the subject adequately.

But for some, the passage of time and life experience is the most helpful thing. In the early years, sex is difficult because the wife is fatigued by childbearing, and the man is inexperienced and insensitive. These factors do change with time.

For the couples who have been married for years, sexual unhappiness can be affected by a renewed relationship with the Lord and putting repentance and forgiveness into effect.

Some couples never quite reach the fullness that they sense is available in marriage. For them, we say that a Christian's measure of happiness and success both as an individual and as a couple does not hinge on achieving sexual heights of pleasure. Thank God that is true. A Christian's worth is evaluated on how well we have loved and cared for our spouse and how well we have loved and served God.

Don't let anyone or anything distort the true set of priorities in a marriage.

To Do This Week

Individual Time

Answer the questions:
1. Have you prayed for your spouse this week?

2. Answer the questions on page 107.

3. Spend time alone with God and repent of any sexual sin from your past life. See page 102.

Time Together

1. Talk about affection honestly—do you greet each other affectionately? Is there affection outside of strictly sexual situations?

2. Share your answers to the questions on page 107.

3. Pray and ask for God's blessing and grace on your sexual relationship. Expect him to bring the two of you closer together in his plan for marriage.

For further reading:

Ed and Gaye Wheat, *Intended for Pleasure* (Old Tappan, N.J.: Fleming H. Revell, 1977).

Tim and Beverly LaHaye, *The Act of Marriage* (Grand Rapids: Zondervan, 1976).

It's OK to Be Different!

ONE OF THE BEST TERMS to describe what it means to love each other is "unity" or "being one." Unity is one of the most powerful concepts of Christian marriage and one of the most misunderstood.

Unity is the Lord's vision for marriage. But unity does *not* mean that the husband and the wife are the *same*.

In the early stage of our relationship, we became aware of how similar we were. We now call this the "Siamese twins" stage. It was that time when we agreed on just about everything—lifestyle, raising children, size of family, money, politics, and everything else. We knew our marriage would be trouble-free. The accent was on "sameness."

Stage two is what we call the "rude awakening." This is the time when you begin to realize how different the two of you really are. You don't really agree about all those areas that you thought you agreed on. He meant one thing and she meant another. You both agreed that your children would be well behaved, but "you can't really expect a one-year-old to be quiet at the dinner table." "When we agreed on living on a tight budget, I didn't mean *never* using a credit card!"

When stage two hits, you can choose to react in discouragement and anger. "What happened to that agreeable girl I married?" or "Whatever happened to that guy who would do anything for me?" Some partners exert a tremendous pressure on each other to return to the "good old days" of sameness. Our experience says that the good old days cannot be repeated, and we are offered a more mature and more *real* way of living together, a way that ultimately is more rewarding and fulfilling than those so-called good old days. Bring on stage three.

Stage three is the one that counts. It is working together toward unity while respecting our differences. Remember: A unity in goal and purpose in life—yes. A unity in raising children—yes. A unity in good financial stewardship—yes. But thinking the same way and liking the same things— no!

Each of us comes to the marriage with a distinct set of experiences and expectations. Where do these differences come from? Let's make a list of the sources of our different expectations:

Parental models	Personal preferences
Upbringing	Sexual differences
Family traditions	Previous experiences with men and women
Economic background	
Ethnic background	Personal strengths and weaknesses
Personality types	

These differences cover most of the formative influences that each of us brings to marriage. They form our expectations of the marriage as a whole as well as specific behavior from our spouse.

Discovering and Dealing with Differences (How Can Two Be One?)

Margaret and Jim have always disagreed about how Margaret treats the children. Jim thinks she yells at the children too much. He also thinks that he and Margaret should not disagree in front of the children but should wait until a time when the children are not around. Margaret can't understand his seeming overconcern with what she calls normal life with young children. She doesn't even consider what she does yelling. She feels Jim misunderstands and judges her too harshly. Jim is frustrated by her lack of concern about something he feels is very important.

Marie and Joe had been married only a short while when they ran head on into an area that has plagued them since. Vacations! Joe is an athletic outdoorsman who thinks a vacation means traveling as far away from civilization as he can, cooking on a camp stove, getting water from a pump, nothing but good old Mother Nature and him. Marie is an active person who thinks a vacation means a hotel room overlooking the ocean, jogging on the boardwalk in the morning, working on her tan, and seeing good plays in the city at night.

Joe doesn't experience hotel life and driving to the city as a rest of any sort. Marie thinks bathing in Lake Superior and drenching herself in mosquito repellant is more like a prison sentence in Siberia than a vacation.

Tension builds every year as summer approaches.

Betty is a gregarious, fun-loving type of woman who is always willing to invite someone over to dinner or to go spontaneously to a movie or party. Her husband, Charlie, a personable fellow on a one-to-one basis in small groups, doesn't feel very comfortable with larger social situations. Dinner for him is a quiet family affair and an evening off is spent in front of the fire with a good book.

We have found that it is very helpful to identify the source or root of differences that couples experience. Often we can interpret resistance on our spouse's part to agree with us as a sign of lack of love, or a lack of commitment to the marriage. If you learn to identify that a source of tension in your marriage springs from different parental models, for example, you can then sit down and deal with it on the level it should be dealt with—family differences rather than a sign of lack of love and commitment.

These types of differences can be resolved in different ways, according to what works best with the two of *you.*

First—you could choose the wife's way of doing things.

Secondly—you could choose the husband's way of doing things.

Thirdly—you can choose a combination of the two ways.

Fourthly—you can start from scratch and design your *own* way.

There is no obviously superior way of working out differences. We find that we use all four ways at one time or another.

One small example for us was Thanksgiving dinner. Randy's mom cooked one type of meal with her unique turkey stuffing while Therese's mom has developed a very different menu over the years. To make a very long story short, we tried *all* four ways of reconciling the differences and have come up with our own Cirner family traditional menu—and a certain tension at each holiday has eased out. We resolved the differences and didn't let those holiday tensions creep in and undermine what is a very joyful time for our family. We're sure that Christmas traditions, family vacations, and chores around the house can be sources of tension for most couples as they were for us.

The key is to take the discussion out of the "you don't want the best for our family" arena and put it into terms that are less explosive and more creatively resolved.

In each of these three cases it helps to understand that *differences* are operating. It is *not* a question of lack of love or lack of commitment. Nor is it a question of who is right and who is wrong. It is a question of two individuals trying to form one life together—the eternal mystery of how *two* can become *one!*

Take the case of Margaret and Jim. Margaret came from a family where yelling and physical contact was the normal way that family members related to each other. Jim came from a very reserved family where it meant big trouble was brewing if his dad or mom raised their voices. Jim saw Margaret's way of relating to the children as wrong behavior that needed correction. Margaret couldn't understand what all the big fuss was about.

Their difference in family background brought conflict to their marriage. Surely some of Margaret's shouting at the children was wrong, and she needed to grow in patience and gentleness with them. She can also learn another way of doing things from Jim and his family, whom she admires.

Understanding that a difference of family experience was the root of the conflict helped them solve this problem in their marriage.

Men! Women!

Men's and women's differences have been the source of jokes as well as pain and misunderstanding. Married people face these differences all the time.

Let's state some of these differences more specifically. This should give us some perspective on how those differences can work together to improve the marriage.

Please bear in mind that these generalizations are imperfect. There are *always* exceptions to the rule. Some qualities are more representative of each sex, but both "masculine" and "feminine" qualities are expressed in both men and women. Finally, the strength of expression of any of these qualities varies tremendously from individual to individual.

Here is a list of qualities or tendencies commonly associated with either men or women.

Women

Tend to relate to themselves as a whole unit—body, mind, emotions

Tend to be sensitive to personal needs

Tend to respond to the immediateness of a situation

Usually desire to bring life and beauty to a situation

Have a strong drive to nurture

Have a strong intuitive sense—the hunch

Usually value how things are related to each other

Respond best sexually when there is an emotional attachment involved

Men

Tend to relate to themselves as separate compartments—a body, a mind, emotions

Tend to have a goal or achievement orientation towards life

Tend to respond to the overall situation and long-term goals

Have a strong aggressive drive

Tend to operate through analysis or ordering things

Distance themselves from situations in order to analyze them

See sex as one of their many activities in life

Who's right? Men and women usually have different reactions to these lists. Here are some typical reactions. "If there are two ways of relating to life, then one is the 'right' way and one is the 'wrong' way." Or: "If God wanted man and woman to get along together, he couldn't have made it more difficult." Or: "So that explains it!"

Focus

Practically, how do these differences look or operate in everyday life? Let's look at some common situations.

Two women were talking at the swimming pool. One described the Olympic sports she had seen on TV the night before. She was filled with visible enthusiasm about gymnastics, volleyball, pole vaulting, and all the other events, except for one. Her whole expression changed with "boxing—ugh!" "Of course," she said, "my husband and son watched boxing, but how they can stand to watch two people try to kill each other is beyond me."

In this situation, several male-female characteristics are operating. The man's capacity for aggressive behavior is exhibited both by the men who are boxing and the men who enjoy watching it. Women say, "How barbaric," because they are projecting themselves into the situation and wondering how anyone can consider it sport to inflict *pain* on someone else. Women usually make some comment about the mental state of people who might enjoy watching two people punch each other.

Men usually don't ask how the boxers must "feel" when they are being hit. They see boxing as a sport where there is an objective set of criteria for the scoring. They admire men who develop the skill of the sport and achieve excellence in it.

Male-female differences in perceiving sports is an example of how men and women may perceive life very differently.

Sometimes women are criticized about how much they talk, especially about other people. There are many jokes and comments and ridicule directed toward women about this area. Women are always on the phone, always interested in other people's lives, always talking.

Women's characteristics help explain this "talkativeness." Because a woman focuses on other persons, she has a strong drive to talk about her life with others. Women usually offer each other a lot of personal support through conversations that can be seen as expressions of the desire to nurture and to give life. It is an expression of the woman's "wholistic" approach to life.

These examples begin to identify sexual characteristics as they operate on a daily basis. "Who's right?" we ask. Often our gut reaction is to think our way is the right way and the other way is wrong. However, both ways, different as they are, are "right."

This is not a joke God played on mankind. In reality, God's reality, he made differences for our good, for the good of all the human race. His arrangement is called "complementarity." Complementarity simply means "to bring to perfection. To complete. Something added to complete a whole." In other words, our lives are *designed* to need both the feminine and the masculine characteristics. Things work best when men are free to be completely men and women are free to be completely women. That's God's wonderful plan. We need to understand how we can make those differences work for us and not against us.

Communication is the springboard for change. You both need to talk about how differences operate in your life. Sometimes just becoming aware of how these qualities affect your life and relationship will relieve tension.

In fact, there very often is a need for mutual *repentance* because of sin in this area. Disrespect, judging, and frustration are common symptoms of sinful behavior or speech.

Respect is the key! Respect how you are similar, and respect how you are different. Some of the healthiest marriages are the ones where mutual respect is a strong quality in the relationship. Statements such as "That's stupid" or in exasperation sighing "Women!" are signs of lack of respect for the differences that each of you have.

Think about how this dynamic of feminine and masculine differences operates in your relationship. Discuss it together. It might be good to also see how these differences operate in your work and family relationships.

Then ask God to give you the insight and the wisdom to approach in a more respectful way the differences you both experience in your marriage.

To Do This Week

Individual Time

Answer the questions:
1. Have I prayed for my spouse and our marriage this week?

2. List at least three ways you can see how masculine and feminine characteristics operate in your marriage.

Time Together

1. Share your answers to question 2 above.

2. Did the two of you experience the three stages of growth described at beginning of the chapter? Are you really in Stage 3, "working together toward unity"?

3. Discuss how differences can express complementarity in your marriage instead of being an obstacle.

Common Obstacles in Marriage

A FTER COUNSELING WITH MANY COUPLES over the last fifteen years, we've noticed some obstacle areas that regularly prevent many couples from enjoying the kind of peace God intended. Here we will choose a few of the more common obstacles and try to offer some general wisdom as well as just plain old common sense.

A Critical or Negative Spirit

We can choose to see either the good and the beautiful in life or the imperfection and the bad in life. One of the most devastating problems in a marriage happens when husband, wife, or both develop a habit of seeing the other person with a critical and negative spirit.

One woman, Kristie, wrote to us about this problem. "From very early on in our married life, I had a very critical and negative attitude toward Steve. Frankly, I didn't like him very much. I concentrated on his faults and

117

shortcomings. I was often depressed and felt very sorry for myself. Here I was, a Christian, and I felt so very little love for my husband.

"After the birth of our third child this depression reached an all-time low. During all these years, I always did what was expected of me—cleaning, cooking, etc.—but I experienced no joy or delight in serving my husband."

Kristie's problem is not unique. Many of us have been trained to have a negative approach to life.

Ray, an executive in his mid-forties, is another example of how a negative approach affects a marriage. He was never satisfied with anything his wife did. It was so bad that he criticized her for even walking into the room the wrong way. Of course by the time they got around to making love, he was very critical of her lack of warmth and responsiveness to him in bed.

There are many reasons why a person develops such a negative response to life—family upbringing, insecurities, defensiveness, habit. The important thing, however, is to work on changing it.

1. Pray and ask God for the help you need. Only through the strength of the Holy Spirit and God's grace can any change happen.

2. See it as a *habit* that you need to break. Criticalness, like other habits, becomes such a part of our daily lives that after a while we fail to notice it.

3. *Decide* that your life and marriage is worth whatever you need to do to change. Set no limits and don't allow any backdoors through which to escape. Believe us, it is worth the effort and energy it will take to break through to victory.

4. *Substitute* positive qualities for the negative ones that you dwell on. Sit down and write on a piece of paper five or ten things that you like or admire in your spouse. Decide to think and speak about those qualities instead of the qualities on the much longer list of 200 things he or she does wrong. This does not mean that the other person all of a sudden starts to do everything right. It does mean that you have decided to choose to notice the good things. Everytime you see or speak with your spouse, instead of the old *habit* of responding critically, choose with the help of God to think and stir up a good and positive perspective.

5. *Other areas* of your life probably work in a similar way. Rarely do we have a difficulty with negativity in only one area of our life. Usually it spills

over into other areas. Examine other areas that might be operating in a similar way. Do your work relationships revolve around comparing yourself to others and concentrating on *their* faults? How about your children? Is the major way you relate to them through criticism? How about yourself?

6. *Comparison* is often the open door to a critical attitude. We habitually compare ourselves to others. We take perverse pleasure when we find someone else lacking. We need to control our thoughts and concentrate on how good God is and be thankful to him for *all* he has given—to others as well as to us.

7. *Scripture* is a key to getting free of a negative attitude. God wants us to fill our minds with his word. Besides daily scripture reading, sometimes it is helpful to take one specific topic and study what God has to say about it. For example, study what scripture says about how we use our minds. Another topic might be gratefulness or the love of God. Use a concordance to help you find the right verses.

Kristie later wrote that she had a significant breakthrough in the area of her attitude toward Steve.

"First I asked some friends that I meet with regularly to pray for me for this problem. Secondly I made a list of ten positive qualities about Steve. Then I thanked God for Steve and each of his good qualities every day during my prayer time. I even discovered more than ten! It has made a tremendous difference in my life and in my personal relationship with Steve.

"Without a superhuman effort on my part, God truly changed my way of thinking about my husband. This new way of thinking generated more personal love and real affection for him. Since I've decided to concentrate on God's grace, on Steve's positive character traits, I can hardly remember the negative anymore (well, almost can't remember!)."

Sometimes both partners are critical and relate negatively toward each other and life in general. In this instance both husband and wife can correct the problem together. Both need to repent and turn to the Lord and ask him for his help. They should make an agreement with each other to not relate through criticism. Then they need to encourage each other to keep the commitments they have made.

Finally, brethren, whatever is true, whatever is honorable, whatever is just, whatever is pure, whatever is lovely, whatever is gracious, if there is any excellence, if there is anything worthy of praise, think about these things. (Phil 4:8)

Self-centeredness and Immaturity

We link immaturity with self-centeredness because we believe that we find true maturity when our lives revolve around others rather than ourselves. Today we are warned that if we don't take care of Number One, no one will. This dire statement is followed by volumes of predictions of all the mental, physical, and sexual disasters that befall the person who doesn't live his life looking out for his own best interests.

Scripture rejects this philosophy. Jesus himself is our model. Scripture says that Jesus is the way to the Father and we should walk that way too. The "me first" mentality is contrary to Christianity.

A self-centered way of life is immature. Infants are totally preoccupied with their own needs. Maturity means growing in awareness of others and the world around us. Full human and spiritual maturity is marked by an increased awareness and an increased concern for the well-being of others.

Unfortunately, our growth in maturity can stop before it should. Some people become adults without making a complete transition from a self-centered to an other-centered approach to life.

This developmental disturbance, coupled with an emphasis on modern "me first" philosophy, can bring difficulty and grief to any marriage. Marriage is for grown-ups. The Christian grown-up is a person who is able to love and serve his or her spouse and children unselfishly.

What can we do about self-centeredness? Here are some steps that work.

1. Identify the problem. Sometimes just reading a section in a book like this will bring about a conviction that "yes, that's me," and that conviction can bring real change. None of us is perfect. Some of that self-concern is in all of us. We all need to go before the Lord and ask him to show us how we are thinking, speaking, and acting in a selfish way.

2. When we begin to see our sin and our self-centeredness, we need to rely on the grace of God. God does not convict us of sin without giving us the full complement of grace for the necessary change.

3. Communicate. We need to begin honestly to relate to one another in

full Christian love and service, confessing our sin, coming before God together, and encouraging one another to do what is right.

4. Decide to be different—in concrete ways. One concrete way of moving out of selfish orientation and *into* an other-centered mode is to make a decision about specific ways you can be different—the right response to conviction of sin is to change that behavior.

A thirty-five-year-old man we know had brought tremendous pain and grief to his wife by demanding that their marriage and family life revolve around what he wanted to do or eat or even talk about. His favorite subject of conversation, naturally, was himself and his concerns.

He decided to change, but his self-centered pattern of life was so ingrained that it was tremendously difficult to be "new." We suggested he start to change in just one or two areas of his life rather than try to tackle everything at once and probably fail.

So he decided to do two things: to ask his wife about her day at dinner each night, and to ask her what she would like to watch on T.V. instead of automatically flipping to his favorite shows. These small but momentous decisions were the beginning of new life and new love in their marriage. As this man opened his eyes to others, he grew in true affection and concern.

What about those nagging self-centered fears, the notion that "If I don't think of myself and my needs, how can I really trust that he or she will love and serve *me*?"

Apply the principles of Christian marriage. Christians aren't perfect. But when both partners are trying to live for God and to live like Jesus, our needs will be met. They may not be met in the way we might *prefer*, but God will provide.

It also helps to distinguish between "needs" and "wants." Sometimes the "wants" are not reasonable or our circumstances are such that it is impossible to fulfill them. Because of human weakness, a husband may not fulfill all his wife's wants. But he can love her and serve her the way the Lord wants.

Discouragement

Scores, hundreds of couples have told us that they had no hope that things could change. "There has been just too much water under the bridge." Too many years, too many hurts, too many problems, too many things said that shouldn't have been said. Too many things that should have been said and weren't. Too many times when I needed her and she let me down. Too many times he walked out.

This is real life, but in another way it is *not* the real life that God wants his people to live.

What do you do if you are discouraged about your marriage? Whether you're young or old, married just for a short time or for fifty years, you need to make a fundamental decision. *Do you want to live the rest of your life in the situation that you're in right now?* You can remain in discouragement, or you can hope in God who is merciful and compassionate and cares for your life and your marriage. "Love bears all things, believes all things, *hopes* all things, endures all things" (1 Cor 13:7).

Whose hope? It is not foolish hope, because our hope is based in God's love. We are tempted to wallow in discouragement and become indifferent to the hope that is offered, but it is *God* who offers, not man. "No, in all these things we are more than conquerors through him who loved us. For I am sure that neither death, nor life, nor angels, nor principalities, nor things present, nor things to come, nor powers, nor height, nor depth, nor anything else in all creation, will be able to separate us from the love of God in Christ Jesus our Lord" (Rom 8:37-39).

We can adapt this passage for discouraged couples: "Neither life, nor death, nor things in the present, nor things in the past, nor things said, nor things not said, nor differences, nor hurts, can separate us from *each other* through the love of God in Christ Jesus our Lord" (paraphrased Cirner version).

Because we hope in God and in his power and his love, we can begin to believe that things can change. Marriages do not change because of our great love or our great power. It is precisely because our resources are insufficient that we need God's love.

Practically, then, what do we do once we decide that we don't want to be discouraged for the rest of our lives?

The first step is for both of you to sit down and decide that neither of you want to continue to live in discouragement. Start to communicate with one another by following the program in this book.

Some difficulties are so complex and communication has broken down so thoroughly in some marriages that the couple should consider marriage counseling. You do need to make sure that the counselor is a Christian. Don't be ashamed of needing some outside help! It is not a sign of failure, but a sign of courage and hope.

Unforgiveness

Unforgiveness has destroyed many marriages. We all sin. Some sin through anger, some sin through infidelity, some through lies or dishonesty or pride. The list of sins that can mar a marriage is long indeed.

Bill was the "injured party." Five years after he and Marie were married she confessed that she had been unfaithful to him once while he was away in the army during the first year of their marriage. She was truly repentant and had great remorse for her sin. She confessed this sin to Bill in response to a call from God to clear sin out of her life and to receive God's forgiveness.

Bill's response was to be horrified, then injured that she had been unfaithful to him. He not only felt he couldn't forgive her, but also became preoccupied with his wife's sin. Ten years later he still brought up her past when he was especially upset. He also was unable to forgive her of the secrecy and dishonesty that accompanied the unfaithfulness.

Of course, Marie had committed a serious sin and Bill had a lot to work through. However, at a certain point all of us need to respond to repentance in the same way that Jesus did—we need to forgive the sinner and to not hold the sin against him.

Unfaithfulness is a dramatic example. There are many smaller ways we can sin against each other—things said in a moment of anger, lies, lack of love, neglect, and many more. We are often tempted to harbor the hurts and keep the hurt or injury alive.

The consequences of keeping injury alive are terrible. Unforgiveness is as destructive to a marriage as cancer is to your body. There is no good in it. There is only death. Christians have only one option—to forgive. We should treat each other in the way God treats us—namely, in forgiveness.

Let's recall how God forgives. When we repent of our sins, admitting that we have done wrong, God forgives us. The sin has been blotted out. It is covered, put from us as far as the east is from the west. Psalm 51 and Psalm 32, as well as passages in the New Testament, give an accurate picture of God's forgiveness. In fact the "Our Father," every Christian's first prayer, says "forgive us our trespasses [sins] as we forgive those who trespass against us."

Hard? Yes. But it is the only response that a Christian can make to a person who asks for forgiveness. The fruit of a forgiving heart is the fruit of the Holy Spirit—joy, peace, and a greater unity in the marriage. It is our pride—a big obstacle indeed—that wants to keep that injury alive. *We* have been hurt; the other one did wrong, not me. Die to pride; die to unforgiveness; die to the perverse pleasure of licking our wounds; and make a new start with your spouse. The grace will be there.

Lack of Communication

Even though we have already devoted a whole chapter to communication, it is worth listing here because lack of it can cause great trouble in a marriage. Often stubbornness, bad habits, and sometimes discouragement make it very difficult to restore communication to what it should be.

Are these the only obstacles to marriage? As Randy once said, "There are as many obstacles in marriage as there are sins for people to commit." Here is a brief list of sins that commonly operate in marriage:

jealousy	manipulation	laziness
envy	materialism	alcohol abuse
lust	guilt	drug addiction
physical abuse	fear	anger
emotional abuse	anxiety	selfishness
pride	fantasy	self-pity
indifference	sexual abuse	lying (deception)
accusation	quarreling	

The Lord's grace and applied Christian wisdom can give each of us the help we all need to triumph over these sins. God has even a greater investment in our lives and our marriages than we do. He loves us and wants the best for all of his people. The promises are there in scripture.

I can do all things in him who strengthens me. (Phil 4:13)

We have not ceased to pray for you, asking that you may . . . live a life worthy of the Lord, fully pleasing to him, bearing fruit in every good work and increasing in the knowledge of God. May you be strengthened with all power, according to his glorious might, for all endurance and patience with joy, giving thanks to the Father, who has qualified us to share in the inheritance of the saints in light.

(Col 1:9-13)

Our journey in marriage is the same one we travel in our personal life with God—our journey is one from darkness into the kingdom of light through the power of the Holy Spirit.

To Do This Week

Individual Time

Answer the questions:
1. Have I prayed for my spouse and our marriage this week?

2. Go through the five major areas listed and ask yourself, "Do *I* have a problem with . . ?"

Time Together

1. Share your responses to the list of areas in question #2 above, with the emphasis on "*I* have a problem. . . ."

2. Discuss how the two of you can support each other in decisions to be "new" in your approach to these obstacles.

3. Review the list of sins on page 124 that can create both small and large obstacles to your marriage.

4. Both get on your knees and ask God's and each other's forgiveness. Accept forgiveness and read Ephesians 4 together.

_____

Postscript
_____

Make Love Your Aim

GOD INTENDS MARRIAGE to be a great joy, not a great trial. Our purpose has been to offer some help on how you can have the joy-filled marriage that both you and God want for you. As we bring to a close our ten weeks "together" we want to say one final thing about marriage—it's an L of a good life. We leave you with some thoughts, all of which begin with the letter L, and capsulize much of what we have shared with you in this book. We think these are the key ingredients in a joyful, Spirit-filled marriage.

Lord. Jesus is the Lord of your marriage. Go to him often in prayer to thank him for what he has done for you and to present your marriage to him. Seek his blessing, his wisdom, his guidance, his power for your life together. Remember, without him, marriage is a risky proposition.

Love. "Make love your aim," Paul says at the beginning of 1 Corinthians 14. Married life is a life of love—God's love—*agape* love. Our aim in marriage is to have our spouse experience God's love through us. Not the up-and-down fickle "love" of the world, but the stable, undying love which seeks the good of our spouse above our own.

Leadership. God's ways in marriage go directly against the grain of current societal concepts of relationship and male and female "liberation." The husband's leadership in marriage, lovingly exercised and lovingly received, is freedom, because true freedom is found in following God. The husband's leadership brings unity, joy, and peace.

Labor. Marriage is a labor of love. It's sometimes hard work, sometimes easy; sometimes routine and boring, sometimes novel and creative; sometimes we feel like it, sometimes we don't; but it's always for our spouse "as unto the Lord."

Listening. "Let [each spouse] be *quick* to hear, *slow* to speak, *slow* to anger" (Jas 1:19). Listening builds love, averts anger, defuses quarrels, brings understanding, is a sign of wisdom.

Laughter. Let the joy of the Lord fill your marriage and let laughter be a part of it. Laughter dispels gloom. Don't take yourselves too seriously or you may become enslaved to rigidity. Joy and laughter are God's gifts to us. Let your marriage enjoy the gift of laughter often.

Loyalty. Let nothing dim your loyalty to one another. Repent of wrongdoing as soon as it happens. Don't speak negatively to one another or about one another to someone else. Encourage and compliment one another. "Outdo one another in showing honor" (Rom 12:10).

Laid-back. Take time to enjoy one another. Don't get so busy that you don't have time for one another. Don't be anxious about the problems in your marriage or the number of changes you may need to make. Deal with them one at a time and be patient. Trust in God and rest in *his* power because you will never do it on your own, anyway.

May God richly bless your marriage. May he lead you ever closer to himself. And may we meet and rejoice together in his everlasting kingdom.

The Weekend

Purpose: There are two main reasons for this weekend. The first is to take time to consolidate some of the things you have been reading about and discussing for the past ten weeks or so and to use what you have begun to implement in your marriage as a base for renewing your marriage commitment. The second purpose of the weekend is for the two of you just to get away from the routines of life and spend some relaxing time together. In short, the weekend is a time for renewal and relaxation.

The actual weekend package we have put together is designed to give you about equal amounts of "work" and relaxation times. We don't think you will find the weekend too heavy.

How to come to the weekend: Both of you should come to the weekend wanting to deepen your relationship and serve each other, not just looking to unwind. If you need a total relaxation weekend, take one, but don't try to do what we have outlined here.

When you leave for the weekend, really leave. As much as possible, leave behind worries or concerns about your business or your home. Let the weekend be a time to focus on your relationship and enjoy each other's company free of interruptions from children, telephone, relatives, work.

What to bring: Usual weekend-away articles. Be sure to include two Bibles—one for each of you and, of course, this book. Bring some recreation items, geared to where you go and what you enjoy.

Time: Friday evening to noon on Sunday.

Friday Evening

After you arrive at your destination and get settled, take a moment to commit the weekend to the Lord and ask his blessing upon it. You can do so in your own words, if you wish, or you can use the prayer below.

Lord Jesus, we thank you for our marriage.

We thank you that we are able to spend this time together.

We place this weekend in your hands and ask that you would be with us to strengthen and refresh us, to deepen our love for you and for one another. Amen.

I. Reread Chapter 1, *Who Is in Charge?*
Discuss with one another the questions:

1. In the last ten weeks, how has *my* understanding of marriage changed?

2. What are the areas of change in our marriage *I* need to concentrate on?

3. What is the one thing that I as your husband (wife) can do to better serve you in our marriage?

After you finish your discussion, it's up to you what you do with the rest of the night.
Before going to sleep read Psalm 23 together.

Saturday Morning

Before you have breakfast give the day to the Lord by reading Psalm 97 together.

I. After breakfast spend some time evaluating the area of communication. It has now been at least three months since you began our suggested approach to communication, and this would be a good time to check with each other on how you think it's going. Here are some questions to help focus the evaluation.

1. How do I think our communication time is going? Check one.
Great ____ Good, but ____ So-So ____ Nonexistent ____
Explain your choice.

2. What do I think *I* can do better in our communication?

3. What are the things my spouse does well in communication? List as many things as you can.

4. What is the *one* thing my spouse can do to better serve our communication?

5. In what areas of our life do we need to be in better communication? When you finish, take some time to do something fun or relaxing.

II. Twenty minutes before lunch sit down and each of you read the book of Colossians; if not the whole book (it's really rather short), at least chapters three and four.

Saturday Afternoon

III. After lunch, talk about what you read in Colossians and how it applies to your marriage. Here are some suggestions to get you started.

1. How conscious am I that I am a new creation in Christ? (Col 3:1-4)

2. What are the things I need to "put to death" in my relationship with my spouse? (3:5ff)

3. What are the two things I need to do a better job of "putting on" in my relationship with my spouse? (3:12ff)

4. Husband: How can I love my wife better? (3:19)

5. Wife: How can I be more submissive to my husband? (3:18)

IV. This would be a good opportunity to be reconciled to one another for past wrongs and sins. You can use the specifics mentioned in Colossians 3 as a starting point. Repent for the things you did wrong, not for everything found in the chapter (unless, of course, you are guilty of them all). Forgive each other directly. Remember how John and Dorothy handled reconciliation in Chapter 3 of this book. Reread it if you need to.

A post-reconciliation embrace and kiss is highly recommended.

Take the rest of the afternoon to do some things you would like: walking, swimming, nap, shopping, sampling the local ice cream parlors.

V. For dinner go out to a nice restaurant and have a leisurely and relaxed meal. Don't talk about anything too heavy, but *do* talk to one another. Spend an enjoyable evening together.

Before going to sleep read Psalm 121 together.

Sunday Morning

Begin the day by giving it to the Lord. Read Psalm 96 together. Go to church services and have breakfast.

I. End the weekend by taking a special time to renew your marriage commitment to one another and to the Lord. We think this is a very appropriate response to the weekend you just had and also to the ten weeks you spent working on your marriage through this book. Renewing your marriage commitment will strengthen the bond of love and unity you both desire for your marriage. For some of you, it can be a new beginning for your marriage. Leave your old married life in that motel room, or cabin, or friend's apartment where you've spent the weekend. Return home to the daily routines of job, house, family as a new married couple empowered by the Holy Spirit to love and serve each other in a new way.

You can renew your marriage commitment in your own words, if you wish. Or you may want to use the promises from your actual wedding ceremony.

Sit or kneel, or stand facing one another as you express your commitment.

Read Psalm 128 together.

Pack and return home.

God bless you.